# CHECHEN-ENGLISH
# ENGLISH-CHECHEN
## DICTIONARY AND PHRASEBOOK

by
NICHOLAS AWDE
and
MUHAMMAD GALAEV

**HIPPOCRENE BOOKS**
*New York*

Hippocrene Books, Inc.
171 Madison Avenue
New York, NY 10016

ISBN 0-7818-0446-9 (pbk.)

Typesetting by Nicholas Awde/Desert♥Hearts

Printed in the United States of America

# CONTENTS

# PREFACE

This guide to conversation is a simple means of sharing the unique Chechen language and culture with speakers of English. It makes no claim to be a linguistic research tool, but is provided as a practical aid for the first steps in communication with an intentionally easy-to-use pronunciation system.

This is the first time Chechen has been presented in such a way, a venture not without its obstacles since the language is still sadly without a truly developed analysis of its structure.

An attempt has been made to provide phrases and scenes from everyday life, as well as items of practical background information, although their relevance clearly will depend on the actual situation in Chechnya.

Thanks to Robert Chenciner for his support in compiling this phrasebook.

- ※ A Chechen person is a **Nokhcho**.
- ※ The adjective for Chechen is **Nokhchi**.
- ※ Chechens call themselves **Vai Nakh** (*see Introduction*) or **Nokhchi Q'am** ('The Chechen People').
- ※ The Chechen language is **Nokhchi Mott**.
- ※ Chechnya is **Nokhchi Mokhk** ('The Chechen Land') or **Nokhchi Chöö** ('The Chechen Area')
- ※ Also heard is **Derstan** ('The Mountain Country'), referring to the traditional heartland of the Chechens. It also means 'Homeland'.
- ※ **Dei Mokhk** means 'Fatherland'.

# INTRODUCTION

The Chechens are an ancient people who have lived on the northern slopes of the Great Caucasus mountain range for thousands of years. After a long history of resistance against the Russians particularly during the 19th century, together with their sister nation the Ingush they came to be an autonomous republic within the USSR in 1934 – the Chechen-Ingush ASSR. The Muslim Chechens call themselves and the Ingush **Vai Nakh** – "Our People", and are presently the largest ethnic group in the North Caucasus.

Constant waves of bloody insurrection against the Russians led to the Chechens being labelled as one of the "treasonous" peoples whose wholesale deportation during World War II was ordered by Stalin – ironically, himself a fellow Caucasian from neighboring Georgia. The deportation in 1944 to Central Asia, the dictator's great Dumping Ground, was ordered in the depth of winter and the loss of life that resulted was predictably appalling. All reference to the Chechen nation and their republic was erased, literally, from every map and book.

Even after Stalin's death and Khruschev's reforms there was opposition to the return of the Chechens and the restoration of their land. But from 1956 onwards, they started to return in small groups, despite still being officially excluded – and often provoking serious clashes with the Russian and Cossack settlers who had taken over their land. Families had to bribe their way back to reclaim their property, until the authorities capitulated and legalised the reversed exodus and the trickle of returnees became a flood. The Soviet government finally gave them back their own autonomous republic in 1957, but with changed borders.

The Chechens have been rebuilding their numbers ever since at a phenomenal rate, with one of the highest birth rates in the ex-Soviet Union, and they now total well over a million in population.

The same year, in the wake of the collapse of the Soviet Union and dissatisfied at their status and treatment in the formation of the new Russian Republic, Chechnya – **Nokhchi Mokhk** – declared itself to be an independent state and seceded. The Russians reacted warily at first, but 1994 saw the inevitable invasion and military occupation of the republic. Sadly, it was the bloody events that followed which have put Chechnya and the Chechens firmly on the world map of today. But their struggle for true recognition still continues.

Chechens are today to be found in all parts of the ex-Soviet Union, especially in the oil industry in Central Asia and Siberia. As a result of the Tsarist campaigns against them in the 19th century, many Chechens left for the lands of the Muslim Ottoman Empire, and consequently significant pockets of Chechens are to be found throughout Turkey and the countries of the Middle East, particularly Jordan.

The Chechen people have maintained their remarkable sense of nationhood through the strength given them by the links of their clans or **teips**, as well as a vibrant Islamic – often Sufi – identity. These links have preserved the Chechens in exile, and restored them to their nation with a structure almost untouched in spite of the atrocities committed against them.

# A VERY BASIC GRAMMAR

Chechen belongs to the Nakh family of languages, which forms part of the group of indigenous languages spoken in the Caucasus – unrelated to any other languages in the world.

The other members of the family are Ingush and Tsova-Tush (or Batsbi). While almost all Chechens speak Chechen as their mother tongue, the majority also speak Russian.

The name 'Chechen' isn't really Chechen at all: it was coined from the name of a village the invading Tsarist armies first encountered. The language has been written since 1923, and presently uses the Cyrillic script.

Throughout history various cultures and peoples have contributed to the vocabulary of Chechen, and mainly the Arabs and the Russians have left their imprint on present-day Chechen in this respect. Chechen was originally only a spoken language and it was subsequently put into a formal writing system by the Soviets, but it is little used in this form.

Until the beginning of this century, Arabic was used principally as the language of written communication. For obvious reasons, Russian has now taken over this role.

## WORD ORDER

While totally unrelated to English – and some of the sounds may at first seem strange – the structure of Chechen is nevertheless quite simple. The verb is usually put at the end of the sentence, e.g.

**So ts'a vööd.**
'I go home.'     (literally: 'I home go')

## NOUNS

Chechen has no words for 'the', 'a' or 'an' – instead the meaning is understood from the context, e.g. **stag** can mean 'the man', 'a man' or just simply 'man'.

Instead of having gender – like in French or Arabic – nouns in Chechen belong to 'classes', which function in a very similar way. Each class originally consisted of nouns which shared similar characteristics: roundness, largeness, length, human, and so on. The class referring to human beings is predictable, the others are not. There are five (or six if you split the first class) such classes. Each triggers a different prefix of agreement in many adjectives and verbs (but not all).

Similar systems exist in languages across the world, such as Chinese, Japanese and Swahili. Here's a basic list showing the forms of the five Chechen noun classes. Remember that these prefixes usually occur in an accompanying verb or adjective– as shown in the examples below – and <u>not</u> in the noun itself:

| CLASS | SINGULAR PREFIX | PLURAL PREFIX | EXAMPLE |
|---|---|---|---|
| 1 | **v-** *for males* | **b-/d-** *for males* | **vasha** brother |
| | **y-** *for females* | **b-/d-** *for females* | **yisha** sister |
| 2 | **y-** | **y-** | **ph'aagal** rabbit |
| 3 | **d-** | **d-** | **latta** earth |
| | | | **beer** child |
| 4 | **b-** | **b-** | **mangal** scythe |
| | **b-** | *nothing* | **malkh** sun |
| 5 | **b-** | **d-** | **mara** nose |

e.g. (*using* **-u** 'is' *and* **-eza** 'heavy'):

| | | | |
|---|---|---|---|
| **Stag** | <u>v</u>eza | <u>v</u>u.* | 'The man is heavy.' |
| **Zuda** | <u>y</u>eza | <u>y</u>u. | 'The woman is heavy.' |
| **Zudari** | <u>b</u>eza | <u>b</u>u. | 'The women are heavy.' |
| **Beera** | <u>b</u>eza | <u>b</u>u. | 'The child is heavy.' |
| **Keema** | <u>d</u>eza | <u>d</u>u. | 'The boat is heavy.' |
| **Bolkha** | <u>b</u>eza | <u>b</u>u. | 'The work is heavy.' |

Note that Class 1 is for humans only ("those with souls"), so there's no harm here in thinking in terms of 'gender', i.e. male and female; but the other classes have lost much of their original classifications and aren't so easy to pigeonhole, so they can be human, animal, vegetable or mineral!

Most nouns form their plural by simply adding **-sh** or **-ash**, e.g. **linz** 'lens' – **linzash** 'lenses'. There are some with irregular plurals, e.g. **ᶜazh** 'apple' – **ᶜeezhash** 'apples', **stag** 'man', 'person' – **nakh** 'people'.

Nouns take a variety of endings. The basic forms with their grammatical descriptions are as follows:

| | |
|---|---|
| Nominative | *no ending* |
| Genitive | **-a(n)** |
| Dative | **-na** |
| Ergative | **-uo/-ye/-s/-a** |
| Instrumental | **-tsa** |
| Locative | **-kh** |
| Comparative | **-l** |
| Allative | **-gaa/-ye** |

Plurals simply add the case endings to the plural marker **-(a)sh**, apart from the Genitive, which ends in **-ii(n)** and the Ergative, which ends in **-a**. The Nominative Plural can also end in **-i** or **-ii**.

As noted above for plurals, some nouns may change slightly according to the form they take (in much the same way as English gives us words like 'goose' and 'geese'), e.g. **ᶜaam** 'lake', **ᶜämnash** 'lakes'.

The Genitive gives us 'of', e.g. **Petima̲i̲i̲(n) televizor** = 'Petima's television' (or 'the television of Petima').

## ADJECTIVES

True adjectives are like nouns in that they decline, but the endings are limited to **-a/-an** in the Nominative singular and plural, and **-achu** in all other cases. They always come before the noun, e.g.

**q'eena** 'old'   **q'eena stag** 'old man'
**zhima** 'young'   **zhima stag** 'young man'

About ten basic adjectives agree with the class of the noun they modify, including (Chechens tend to use the female **y-** prefix as the 'neutral' form):

**yay** light   **yowkha** hot
**yeza** heavy   **yüq'a** thick
**yoqqa** elder   **yutq'a** thin

e.g.   <u>y</u>eza k'ant   'heavy boy'*
       <u>y</u>eza yakhka   'heavy box'

## ADVERBS

Most adverbs have one single form which never changes. Some examples:

**dika(n)** well   **d<sup>c</sup>a** there
**vwo(n)** badly   **hintsa** now
**hoquzah'** here   **qaana** tomorrow

Most adjectives can be used as an adverb.

## POSTPOSITIONS

Chechen has postpositions, in other words words like 'in', 'at' and 'behind' come <u>after</u> the noun and not before it as in English (although remember that you can say 'who *with*?' as well as '*with* who?' – and there's no change in meaning). They generally take the dative or nominative case.

**aara** out   **k'yela** under
**chu** in, into   **t'äh'a** after
**h'alkha** in front of   **t'eeh'a** behind
**lätsna** about   **t'ye** on
**metta** instead of   **yuq'a** in the middle of

But the sense of English prepositions is more

* This also means 'dear boy'.

often rendered by the 'preverbs' (see below in Verbs).

## PRONOUNS

Personal pronouns take case endings. Basic forms are as follows:

| SINGULAR | | PLURAL | |
|---|---|---|---|
| **so** | I | **tkho** | we *exclusive* |
| | | **vai** | we *inclusive* |
| **h'o** | you *singular* | **shu** | you *plural* |
| **i; iza** | he/she/it | **üsh; üzash** | they |

Note that there are two forms for the single English word 'we'. The exclusive **tkho** means 'us only (and not them)', while the inclusive **vai** means 'us all'.

Possessive pronouns are formed by using the genitive of the personal pronoun:

| SINGULAR | | PLURAL | |
|---|---|---|---|
| **sa** | my | **tkha** | our *exclusive* |
| | | **vai** | our *inclusive* |
| **h'a** | your *singular* | **shu** | your *plural* |
| **tsüna** | his/her/its | **tseera** | their |

Demonstratives are as follows:

| | | | |
|---|---|---|---|
| **hara** | this | **hworsh** | these |
| **dᶜaaranig** | that | **dᶜaaranash** | those |

## VERBS

As in English, verbs change their form according to tense only and the same form is used for all singular and plural persons. About one third of all verbs, however, will make an additional change for the <u>class</u> (and not person) of the subject, e.g.

| | |
|---|---|
| **Stag aara <u>v</u>eelira.** | The man went out. |
| **Beer aara <u>d</u>eelira.** | The child went out. |

The simple infinitive ends in **-a(n)**, e.g. **daakha(n)** 'to live.' By changing endings, there are seven basic tenses, as well as a variety of compound tenses. Since Chechen has only a few hundred true verbs and cannot create any more, nouns are used with the verb **dan** 'to do' to create phrasal verbs.

Like nouns, some verbs may change spelling slightly according to the form they take (like English 'kn<u>o</u>w' and 'kn<u>e</u>w'), e.g. **mala(n)** 'to drink', **molu** 'drinks'.

The negative is formed by putting **tsa** 'not' immediately before the verb. **Ma** 'do not' is used with commands.

Postpositions are used with verbs (and so are called 'preverbs') to add to the meaning.

| | |
|---|---|
| **d<sup>c</sup>a** there | **chu** in |
| **s'h'a** here | **aara** out |
| **h'ala** up | **t'ye** on |
| **(w)oh'a** down | **bukha** under |
| **vowshakh** each other | |

The verb 'to have' is usually expressed using the verb 'to be', e.g. **Ts'h'ana voqqachu stega qwo' k'ant khilla.** 'An old man had three sons' – this translates literally as 'There were three boys to an old man.'

# PRONUNCIATION GUIDE

| Chechen letter | Chechen example | Approximate English equivalent |
|---|---|---|
| ' | **ha'** 'yes' | — |
| a | **akhcha** 'money' | short: p**a**t |
| | **aara** 'out' | long: f**a**ther |
| ä | **ärroo** 'left' | — |
| b | **bashkhan** 'excellent' | **b**ox |
| ch | **chai** 'tea' | **ch**urch |
| ch' | **ch'oogha** 'strong' | — |
| d | **daakhar** 'life' | **d**og |
| e | **eskar** 'army' | short: p**e**t |
| | **eetsa** 'to buy' | long: like the **a** in p**ai**d |
| f | **futbol** 'soccer' | **f**at |
| g | **geena** 'far' | **g**et |
| gh | **ghala** 'town' | — |
| h | **haa-ha'** 'no' | **h**at |
| h' | **h'aasha** 'visitor' | — |
| i | **iza** 'he, she, it' | short: s**i**t |
| | **niisa** 'straight' | long: s**ea**t |
| j | **jaz** 'jazz' | **j**et |
| k | **kellä** 'new' | **k**ick |
| k' | **k'ai** 'white' | — |
| kh | **khi** 'water' | lo**ch**, as in Scottish English |
| l | **la'amalla** 'independence' | **l**et |
| m | **ma** 'do not' | **m**at |
| n | **nana** 'mother' | **n**et |
| o | **ofis** 'office' | short: c**o**t |
| | **ooramat** 'crops' | long: c**oa**t |
| ö | **özda** 'polite' | — |
| p | **prezident** 'president' | **p**et |

| | | |
|---|---|---|
| **p'** | **P'eerska** 'Friday' | — |
| **q** | **qo'** 'three' | — |
| **q'** | **q'u** 'thief' | — |
| **r** | **reeza** 'happy' | *r*at, but 'rolled' as in Scottish English |
| **s** | **sah't** 'hour' | *s*it |
| **sh** | **sha** 'ice' | *sh*ut |
| **t** | **tüka** 'shop' | *t*en |
| **t'** | **t'elatar** 'invasion' | — |
| **ts** | **tsul** 'more' | hi*ts* |
| **ts'** | **ts'eeno** 'house' | — |
| **u** | **uggar** 'most' | short: p*u*t |
| | **uuram** 'street' | long: sh*oo*t |
| **ü** | **üsh** 'they' | — |
| **v** | **vasha** 'brother' | *v*an |
| **w** | **wu** 'he/it is' | *w*in |
| **y** | **yu** 'she/it is' | *y*es |
| **z** | **zuda** 'woman' | *z*ebra |
| **zh** | **zhim** 'small' | era*z*ure |
| **c** | **<sup>c</sup>an** 'winter' | — |

Nothing beats listening to a native speaker, but the following notes should help give you some idea of how to pronounce the following letters.

## VOWELS

The general difference in length of vowels is important, e.g. **d<u>a</u>la** 'to give' — **d<u>aa</u>la** 'to end'.

The following vowels are 'umlauted', and have similar pronunciation to German or Turkish *ä, ö* and *ü*:

**ä** is like the 'a' in 'pat', but with a quality closer to 'pet' than 'part'. **ää** is pronounced twice as long.

**ö** has a similar sound to the vowels in 'her' or 'stir', but without any 'r' and with pointed and narrowly rounded lips. **öö** is pronounced twice as long.

**ü** has a similar sound to the vowel in 'huge' but much shorter. Another way of producing this is to say 'kiss' but with pointed and narrowly rounded lips, so that the 'i' almost becomes a 'u'. **üü** is pronounced twice as long.

All vowels can be nasalized, e.g. 'to drink' can be heard as **mala** or **mala_n_**.

## CONSONANTS

**ts** Note that this, as in other Caucasian languages and Russian, represents a *single* sound.

**ch', k', p', q', k', t'** and **ts'** are all *glottalised* versions of **ch, k, p, q, k, t** and **ts** respectively. You may also hear them referred to as *ejective* consonants. These terms simply mean that each consonant's basic sound is modified in a similar way to produce a less breathy, 'harder' version. As an example, begin making the sound **k** as you normally would, but momentarily stop the breath going into your mouth by closing the fleshy bits (your glottis) at the very back. Hold your tongue and lips in the position they should be in to pronounce the **k** and then suddenly pronounce it. Rather than let out a stream of breath with the sound there should be instead an 'explosion' simultaneously accompanying the sound. At first you may find it easier to do this for consonants at the ends of words.

**'** is what is called the 'glottal stop'. You simply close the glottis at the very back of mouth/top of your throat, and then release the built up air. The result is a light 'uh' sound with a very slight grunt just before it. Although it's not written, it occurs in the conversational speech of nearly all

English speakers, being most noticeable in the pronunciation of words like "bottle" as "bo'el" by many Londoners. Since this sound is pronounced predictably before every word beginning with a vowel it's not necessary to mark it in this book. [= Arabic ء]

**h'** is a more emphatic form of **h**. Take the exhaling sound you make when you've just burnt your mouth after taking a sip of boiling hot soup, push it right back into the very back of your mouth, making sure your tongue goes back too, and that should give a good approximation! [= Arabic ح]

**c** if you follow the same pronunciation rules for **h'**, with your tongue and back of mouth all pressed up against the back of your throat, then simply change the hiss of the **h** to a sound using your vocal cords. If you're then sounding like you're being choked, then you've got it. Hint: Rather than think of **c** as a consonant, think of it as a 'vowel modifier', and when listening to a native speaker, note how it changes any vowel in its vicinity, 'pharyngealizing' the vowel, sending half the sound up the nose. [= Arabic ع]

**q** is pronounced like a **k**, but right back in your mouth at the throat end, in the same area as **h'** and **c**. Imagine you have a marble in the back of your throat and that you're bouncing it using only your glottis, and make a **k** sound at the same time. [= Arabic ق]

**gh** is pronounced like a sort of growl in the back of yourr throat—like when you're gargling. The German or Parisian 'r' is the easy European equivalent. [= Arabic غ]

**kh** is the rasping 'ch' in Sottish 'loch' and German 'ach'. It is also pronounced like the Spanish/Castillian 'jota'. [= Arabic خ]

1) In many cases **z** alternates with **dz**, **v** with **w**, **gh** with **kh**, and **zh** with **j** without change of meaning.

2) Consonants can be 'doubled', e.g. **mellish** 'slow' is pronounced very distinctly as **mel-lish**.

3) Many speakers will vary their pronunciation by either adding or subtracting a **y** or **w** before many vowels, e.g. 'Chechen' can be pronounced as **Nokhchi** or **Nwokhchi**, 'house' as **ts'eeno** or **ts'yeeno**.

4) Chechens are very relaxed over how they end words, e.g. 'to do' is **dan**, which can also be written and pronounced as **da**, which itself is more often than not pronounced as plain **'duh'**; 'small' is **zhim** or **zhima**, and generally pronounced **'zhim-uh'**.

5) Very much like in English, the consonants and especially vowels of Chechen vary widely from area to area. The official alphabet, needless to say, doesn't reflect any of these variations. Many words and expressions, too, which are obviously borrowed from Russian will tend to vary between Russian and Chechen pronunciations, depending on the speakers and the circumstances. Don't be surprised if many speakers suddenly switch into Russian mid-sentence. Russian words (and a growing number of English ones, too) are especially used in areas such as politics, science or technology.

6) The sequence **ow** is pronounced like English 'toe'.

7) An apostrophe is used in **s'h** and **ts'h** in order to avoid confusion between the single sound **sh** and the two sequences of **s** plus **h**, and **ts** plus **h**.

8) As described in the Grammar section, the class system triggers changes at the beginnings of many words. The most common alternation you will find in this book is **w-** or **v-** for males referred to, and **y-** for females referred to, e.g. **'So Avstraliera wu/yu'** 'I am from Australia' means that you say **'so Avstraliera wu'** if you are <u>male</u>, and **'so Avstraliera yu'** if you are <u>female</u>. Frequent alternations are: **wu/yu, wui/yui, vella/yella, veeza/yeeza, wats/yats, wälla/yälla, verza/yerza**. The distinction for these will not be noted in the text beyond the presence of the slash mark.

9) Abbreviations used are: *m* for 'male' and *f* for 'female'.

# THE CHECHEN ALPHABET

| Chechen letter | | Chechen name of letter | Chechen letter | | Chechen name of letter |
|---|---|---|---|---|---|
| А | а | [a] | Т | т | [te] |
| Аь | аь | [ä] | ТӀ | тӀ | [t'a] |
| Б | б | [be] | У | у | [u] |
| В | в | [ve] | Уь | уь | [ü] |
| Г | г | [ge] | Ф | ф | [ef] |
| ГӀ | гӀ | [gha] | Х | х | [kha] |
| Д | д | [de] | Хь | хь | [h'a] |
| Е | е | [ee] | ХӀ | хӀ | [ha] |
| Ё | ё | [yo] | Ц | ц | [tse] |
| Ж | ж | [zhe | ЦӀ | цӀ | [ts'a] |
| З | з | [ze] | Ч | ч | [che] |
| И | и | [ii] | ЧӀ | чӀ | [ch'a] |
| Й | й | [dotsa ii] | Ш | ш | [sha] |
| К | к | [ka] | Щ | щ | [shcha] |
| Кх | кх | [qa] | | ъ | [ch'ogha khaark] |
| Къ | къ | [q'a] | | | |
| КӀ | кӀ | [k'a] | | ы | [i] |
| Л | л | [el] | | ь | [k'eda khaark] |
| М | м | [em] | | | |
| Н | н | [en] | Э | э | [e] |
| О | о | [o] | Ю | ю | [yu] |
| Оь | оь | [ö] | Юь | юь | [yü] |
| П | п | [pe] | Я | я | [ya] |
| ПӀ | пӀ | [p'a] | Яь | яь | [yä] |
| Р | р | [er] | Ӏ | Ӏ | [ᶜa] |
| С | с | [es] | | | |

# CHECHEN
## DICTIONARY

# CHECHEN-ENGLISH
## NOKHCHII-INGALS

## A Ä <sup>c</sup>

**a** and

**<sup>c</sup>a** winter; **<sup>c</sup>a yuqqe** midwinter

**Abkhaz** Abkhaz

**ächka neq'** railway

**adam** person

**adamin baq'oonash** human rights

**adapter** adapter

**<sup>c</sup>a dika yöila** goodbye

**administrator** manager

**adres** address

**advokat** lawyer

**aeroport** airport

**aeroporta(n) nalog** airport tax

**agronom** agronomist

**ah'a** grind

**ai'a(n): h'ala 'ai'a(n)** to lift up

**<sup>c</sup>aig** (*plural* **<sup>c</sup>aigash**) spoon

**aighar** stallion

**akademi** academy

**akh** one-half

**<sup>c</sup>aakhar** lamb

**aakhar-latta** fallowland

**akhcha** money; coins; **akhcha dala** pay; **akhcha khiitsar** exchange; **akhcha khötsurg (lush bolu makh)** commission; **akhcha(n) keekhatash** bank notes

**aakharkho; aakharkhwo** farmer; peasant

**akhka** to dig; to plow

**ächhkee** summer

**ächhkee yuqq'a** midsummer

**akumulyator** battery

**akusherka** midwife

**<sup>c</sup>aaläm** world

**<sup>c</sup>aalama(n) bookham** natural disaster

**ala(n); aala(n)** to say; to tell; to sing

**alergii: Sa . . .-na alergii yu.** I'm allergic to . . .

**aalina** having said; that

**alkagolik** alcoholic

**alkagolizm** alcoholism

**alkogol** alcohol

**älla** having said; that

**allergii** allergy

**alsamoo** more

**<sup>c</sup>aam** (*plural* **<sup>c</sup>ämnash**) lake

**<sup>c</sup>aama(n)** to learn

**ambar** barn

**Amerika** America; USA

**Amerikanets; Amerikanski; Amerikii** American

**amma** but

**<sup>c</sup>aamoo** to teach

**amputatsi** amputation

**<sup>c</sup>a(n)** winter; **<sup>c</sup>a(n) yuqq'e** midwinter

**analgin** painkiller

**<sup>c</sup>aana(n)** to pour out; to spill

**anasteziiya** anesthetic

**anastezist** anesthetist

**anemia** anemia

**Anglii** Britain; British; England; English

**antibiotik** antibiotic

**antibiotikash** antibiotics

**antifriz** anti-freeze

**antiseptik** antiseptic

**apelsin** orange
**apenditsiit** appendicitis
**Aprel** April
**apteka** pharmacy
**aaqa(n)** wild
**aara** out; **aara daala(n)** to go out
**aaradaqqa** withdraw
**aaradovliila** exit
**ᶜArbii(n)** Arabic
**aare** field; plain
**arkheologicheski** archaeological
**arkhitektor** architect
**armi** army
**ärroo** left
**ärroo aagho** left-hand
**ärrooh'ara** left-wing
**arteri** artery
**artileri** artillery
**ᶜärzha** black; dark
**ᶜärzhi-k'ai** B&W (film)
**ärzu** eagle
**as-salaamu ᶜalaikum** hello
**äshpash** lies
**äshpash bitta(n)** to tell lies
**aspirin** aspirin
**astma** asthmatic
**atlas** atlas
**atletika** athletics
**ätta(n)** easy
**ᶜätta: So ᶜätta vina/yina.** I have been vomiting.
**ättoo** right; success
**ättoo aagho** right-hand
**ättooh'ara** right-wing
**ättoo tsa khilar** failure
**avarii** emergency; accident
**avariini aaradovliila** emergency exit
**Avgust** August
**aviya poshta** air mail
**Avstrali** Australia
**Avstralii(n)** Australian
**avtobus** bus

**avtobusa(n) ostanovka** bus stop
**avtomat** machine gun
**avtonomi** autonomy
**avtovogzal** bus station
**aaz** voice
**Azerbaijanii(n)** Azeri
**ᶜazap** torment; torture
**ᶜazh** (plural **ᶜeezhash**) apple

# B

**baakham** farm
**baarhiitta** eighteen
**baarz** grave
**baazar** market
**bächcha** leader
**badd** duck
**baga khi qorzurg** mouthwash
**bagazhni sektsi** baggage counter
**bagazhnik** boot
**bak** tank
**bakteresh** germs
**bakteriya** bacteria
**balda** lip
**Balkarii(n)** Balkar
**balkon** balcony
**bamba** cotton; cotton wool
**bamper** bumper
**bandit** gangster
**bank** bank
**banka** can
**baq'oo** right
**baq'derg** truth
**baq'o yala** to let; to allow
**bar** bar
**bᶜaar** nut
**baaramäh'** size
**bᶜärg** eye
**bᶜärgekh khiish ökhiita gaz** tear gas
**barkalla** thank you; thanks; **As barkalla booghu.** I am grateful.

**barkalla baakha(n)** to thank

**barkh** eight

**b<sup>c</sup>ärkhi** tear (*from eye*)

**b<sup>c</sup>är sa** eyesight

**b<sup>c</sup>arza** mule

**b<sup>c</sup>ärzee** blind

**basäh'** in color

**b<sup>c</sup>ästee** spring

**basar** paint

**base** slope

**bashkha(n)** excellent

**basketbol** basketball

**batarei** battery

**bätstsara(n)** green

**batt** mouth

**bazha** herd

**b<sup>c</sup>ee** hundred; **b<sup>c</sup>e sho / be<sup>c</sup> sho** century

**bekhka** debt; obligation

**bekhkam ban** to forbid

**bekhkaza(n)** innocent

**bekhk ma billalah'** excuse me; sorry

**belkhi** aid; mutual aid

**bell** spade

**belsh** shoulder

**benzin** gas; fuel

**benzina(n) sklad** fuel dump

**beepig** bread

**beepig dottu mettig** bakery

**beer** child

**beer(a) dar** birth

**beera dara(n)** give birth

**beera(n) ts'a** womb

**beerakh: So beerakh yu.** I'm pregnant.

**beerash** children

**berhiitta** eighteen

**besa(n)** pale; colorless

**besh** orchard

**b<sup>c</sup>e sho; be<sup>c</sup> sho** century

**bezhana(n) zhizhig** beef

**bezhenets** refugee

**bezhentsash** refugees

**bh'aagor: Suuna bh'aagor hiiza.** I feel dizzy.

**bibliyotechni** (*adjective*) library

**bibliyoteka** library

**bilet** ticket

**bileta(n) kassa** travel agent

**binokal** binoculars

**bint** bandaid

**bitta(n): äshpash bitta(n)** to tell a lie

**b<sup>c</sup>izh** illegitimate child

**biznis** business

**biznismen** business person

**blok** carton

**blokpost** roadblock

**bluuz** blues

**boda** (*noun*) dark

**boh'; böh'** peak; summit; top

**boida neekha lager** refugee camp

**böögha; böökha** dirty

**bookham** disaster

**bookhush** saying; that

**bokhcha** wallet

**bölak** copse

**bolat** steel

**bolkh** work; **H'o hu bolkh besh wu?** What do you do?

**bolkh ba(n)** to work

**bolkh oh'atasar** strike

**bolnitsa; bolnitsi** hospital; clinic

**bomba** bomb

**bombardirovka** air raid; bombardment

**bombardirovshik** bomber

**bomba zeenaz ya** bomb disposal

**böömasha** brown

**boqqa mänga** double bed

**boqqa p'elg** thumb

**börsha** male

**borz** wolf

**bos** color
**bos bolu plyonka** color (film)
**bozhal** barn
**braslet** bracelet
**bron** reservation
**broshka** brooch
**B.T.R.** armored car
**Buddist** Buddhist
**Buddizm** Buddhism
**bugha** bottom
**buha** owl
**bui?** is there?/are there?
**büisa** night
**büisana yuq'** midnight
**bukha** under
**bukhara(n)** lower
**bukhgalter** accountant
**buksira(n) mush** tow rope
**bunt** riot
**büökha(n)** dirty
**bwolkh** work
**buq'a** back
**buq'a lazar/ann** backache
**burak** beetroot
**buram** ferry
**burch** pepper
**bürk** ball
**burts** pepper
**Busurba dina** Islam
**Busurban** Muslim
**buts** grass
**butt** month; moon; **butt buzar** full moon; **butt ts'inbaalar** new moon
**butuolag** stocky person
**büüda(n)** raw
**bwolkh** work
**bworts** millet
**bworz** wolf
**byerch** callus
**byerd** river bank

# C CH CH'

**cha** (*plural* **cherchii**) bear
**chai** tea; **limon tesna chai** tea with lemon; **shura tökhna chai** tea with milk
**chaink** kettle
**chakhcha(n)** to burn: to get burned
**chaamaz** tasteless
**cham bolush** tasty
**chamda** suitcase
**ch'ᶜara** fish
**chashka** cup
**ch'eeᶜa** crybaby
**chᶜeeri liitsa** fishing
**ch'enga** chin
**cheqq daalar** end
**Chergazii(n)** Circassian
**cherma** cask
**chetar** parachute
**ch'h'äwrig** cockroach
**chh'woch** fool
**chiilik** bucket
**chimtosurg** ashtray
**chirq** lamp
**chöö** room; **chöön nomer** room number
**ch'oogha** strong; hard; serious; very
**chööh'a waala/yaala!** come in!
**choh' lazar** diarrhea
**chöh'aara kema/reis** internal flight
**chöö** interior
**chöö lozu** stomachache
**choo yan** wound
**chorpa** soup
**chow** trauma; wound
**chow dh'a teegar** (surgical) stitches

# Dekabar

**chow ďh'a yerzosh molkha**
antiseptic
**choo yuq'a** constipation
**ch'ozh** ravine
**chu** in; into
**ch'ug** ring
**chughoila** entrance
**chukhchari** waterfall
**chükhol yuugha humnash**
underwear
**ch'uuram** candle
**ch'uuramhottorg** candlestick
**ch'urg** tire; wheel; **Sa ch'urg
iqqan.** I have a puncture.
**chürk** mosquito
**chyorni rinok** black market

# D

**da(n)** father
**dᶜa** there
**däᶜakhk** bone
**da'a nana'a dootsush beera**
orphan
**dada(n)** to run; to flee
**dᶜagakhula** that way
**daga dan** to remember
**daagar** fever; temperature
**daago** burn
**daago dechig** firewood
**dah'a** ride
**dah'a dar** frostbite
**dah'iita** send
**däh'nii** cattle
**dai'a(n)** lose
**dain** cheap; light (in weight)
**daakha(n)** to live; to dwell
**daakhar** life
**dakhka** mouse
**daakhka(n)** to be contained; to
be located
**daala** (noun) light

**dala(n)** to give
**daala(n)** to tread; to arrive; to
enter
**dalar** death
**dälla: Mas dälla wain?** What time
is it?
**da(n)** (noun) father; (verb) to
cause; to do; to make
**dᶜändarg** bullet
**daaq'a** portion; share; part
**daqqa(n)** to take; to deprive; to
get; to win
**dᶜaq'owla** to close
**dᶜaaranash** those
**dᶜaaranig** that
**darsta(n)** to get fat
**darts** blizzard
**darzha(n)** to spread (out); to
extend; to spill; to get murky
**därzhna** murky; extended
**dᶜaasadiga** to transport; to
deliver
**dasswo** to empty; to drain
**Datkhoi(n)** Danish
**daat'a(n)** to split; to explode
**dätta** oil
**dätta(n) kanistar** oilcan
**davleni: logha/leqa davleni**
low/high blood pressure
**day'a** to spend; to lose
**de** date; day; daytime; **Takhana
hu de du?** What's the date
today?; **di' de dälcha** four days
from now; **di' de h'algha** four
days before
**de'a deeq'akh qo'a** three-quarters
**dechig** wood
**dechig-ph'ar** carpenter
**dega pkha** artery; vein
**degh** body
**dei büüsi** day (24 hours)
**deitta** fourteen
**Dekabar** December

**deekha(n)** to cost
**Deela** God
**delkha** weep
**delq'a kha(n)** noon
**delq'a kha(n) t'iah'** afternoon; in the afternoon
**delq'a(n) yu'urg** lunch
**demokrati** democracy
**demoktii(n)** democratic
**demonstrant** (*political*) demonstrator
**demonstratsi** (*political*) demonstration
**de(n)** (*noun*) day; (*verb*) to sow; to murder
**de(n) da(n)** (*paternal*) grandfather
**de(n) nana** (*paternal*) grandmother
**depo** depot
**deportatsi** deportation
**deeqar** debt
**deer** death; murder
**deera(n)** angry
**derrig 'a** (*singular*) all; a whole
**derstana** fat
**deesa(n)** empty
**deesa latta** wasteland
**desert** dessert
**deeshash dolu loo** sleet
**deshi** gold
**desta** swell
**deti** silver
**detta** to ring
**deza** expensive; heavy
**dezodorant** deodorant
**dh'a daghnacha k'irnah'** last week
**dh'a daqqar** cancellation
**dh'a vaala (balkhar)** to quit (one's job)
**dh'a vagha bilet** one-way ticket
**dh'a waalah' quzar!** go away!
**dh'a wööda de** date of departure

**dh'a yai'a(n)** switch off
**dh'adaghar** departures
**dh'ai-s'h'ai vagha bilet** return ticket
**di'** four
**diabet** diabetic
**dig** axe
**diga(n)** to lead; to guide; to take to
**dika(n)** well; good; fine; **dikakh** better, **uggar dika(n)** the best
**dikanig** good one!
**dikkakh** even better
**diktator** dictator
**diktatura** dictatorship
**dila(n)** to put
**dilla** to draw; to lay; to put
**dillana** open
**din** religion
**diina(n)** alive
**diinat** animal
**diplomat** diplomat
**diplomatin yuq'amettigash** diplomatic ties
**dita(n)** to leave
**diitsa(n)** to say
**diitsar dillar** discussion
**dits da(n)** to forget
**diizel** diesel
**direktor** manager
**disk-jokei** disk jockey
**diskoteka** disco
**ditt** tree; wood
**diyagnoz** diagnosis
**diyeta** diet
**do<sup>c</sup>ah'** liver
**dö'algha** fourth; **dö'algha daaq'a** one-quarter
**dog** heart; **dog ghiila khilar** heart condition
**dogha** rain; **dogha doogha** it is raining

**doogha** key; padlock; lock; raining

**dogovor** agreement

**dogovor k'el küg ta<sup>c</sup>o** to sign an agreement

**döhh'al** opposite

**döhh'ar** first

**dokhk** mist; fog; **dokhk dolush** misty; foggy

**dökhk** belt

**dokhka** (*adjective*) misty; foggy; (*verb*) to sell

**dökhka** (*medical*) sling

**doklad** report

**dokladkho** speaker

**dokument** identification

**dokumentalni** documentary

**dollar** dollar

**dolush** included

**domkrat** jack

**dootsu** short

**dootsush** excluded

**dow** feud; dispute; quarrel

**dow khattar** trial

**dooza** border

**doozanal deeh'avaalar** border crossing

**dööztq'a** eighty

**dööztq'ee 'itt** ninety

**dopolnitelni nomer** extension

**doq'ar** (*noun*) feed

**doqalla** level

**doqqa** big

**doqqa khiila** grow up

**dorozhni cheekash** travelers' checks

**dottagh** friend

**dowgha(n); dowkha(n)** hot

**dowkha khi** hot water

**dowkha** warm

**dowza(n)** to know (*someone*)

**dözal** family

**dözal khilar** marital status

**drel** drill

**duga** rice

**duh'al khiilar** protest

**düh'al khiila(n)** to protest

**dui?** there: is there?/ are there?

**duqa duqa** too much

**duqa kezzig/zhima** too little

**dukhi** perfume

**dünya** world

**duq'** pass: mountain pass

**duqa** a lot; many; more

**düq'a(n)** thick (*dense*)

**duqa-duqa** many: (too) many/much

**duqakha derg** majority

**duqqa duqa** too much

**düra(n)** salty

**dush** shower

**d<sup>c</sup>üüt'a** giant

**dutq'a(n)** thin

**duukha(n)** to put on; to dress; to wear

**duza(n)** fill

**dwog** heart

**dwogh** rain

**dwolo** to begin

**dwottagh** friend

**dyekha(n); dyekhar da(n)** to ask

**dyelkha(n)** to cry

**dyesha(n)** to read

**dyeshar** reading; study

**dyeza(n)** to like; to love

**dyeztq'a** eighty

**dyeztq'ee 'itt** ninety

# E

**echig** iron

**<sup>c</sup>eedal** regime

**ekkha** to blow up

**ekonomist** economist

**eksponometr** light meter

**elekrotovarsh dukhka tüka**
electrical goods store
**elektrichestvo** electricity
**elektrobigudi** heating coil
**elektroni pochta** e-mail
**e-mail** e-mail
**emall** enamel
**epidemi** epidemic
**epilepsi** epileptic
**epsar** officer
**eqqar** explosion
**eqqaz yolu bomba** unexploded
bomb
**Ermaloi(n); Ermloi(n)** Armenian
**erza** tower
**eesa** calf
**eskar** army
**etazh** floor
**etkash** boots
**etmä<sup>c</sup>ig** snail
**etnicheski chistka** ethnic cleansing
**eetsa** buy
**eetsina** brought
**ewlyaa'a** saint
**ewlyaa'a(n) kash** saint's tomb
**ezar** thousand

# F

**fabrika** factory
**faks** fax
**famili** surname
**fen** hairdryer
**ferma** farm
**fermer** farmer
**Fevral** February
**filter yolu** filtered
**filter yotsush** filterless
**fizeyoterapi(ya)** physiotherapy
**fonarik** flashlight
**fonarr lat yan** to shine a light
**forma** uniform

**foto aparat** camera
**frank** franc
**Frantsuzii(n)** French
**funt sterling** sterling
**fut** foot
**futbol** soccer
**futboli mach** soccer match
**fyoletovi** purple

# G GH

**gai** womb
**gaita(n)** to show
**galerei** art gallery
**gali** sack
**gallon** gallon
**galmorze** crossroads
**galstuk** necktie
**ga(n)** to see
**gangrena** gangrene
**gangster** gangster
**-gar(a)** from
**garam** gram
**garnizon** garrison
**garznash** pasta
**gata** scarf; towel
**gaaza** goat
**gaz balon** butane canister
**gaz pedal** accelerator
**gazet** newspaper
**gazoprovod** gas pipeline
**geena** far; far away
**geenah'** far
**genekolog** gynecologist
**gennara(n)** distant
**gerga** more or less
**gergara (stag/zuda)** relative
(male/female)
**gerza(n) sklad** arms dump
**gezg** spider
**ghaiba** pillow
**Ghaazaqii(n)** Russian

**ghaighanii** sad

**ghaala** castle; fort; town; city; tower

**Ghaala** Grozny

**ghaalat** mistake

**ghaalat daala(n)** to make a mistake

**ghalii(n) yuqqa** town center; main square

**Ghalghai** Ingush

**ghaalin karta** city map

**ghalii(n) yuqq'e** town center; main square

**Ghalmaqii** Kalmuk

**ghammagha** peach

**gha(n)** dream

**ghant** chair

**ghaz** goose

**Gheebartoi** Kabardian

**ghiila** weak

**ghirs** equipment; gear; stuff

**ghishlo** temple; building

**gho(n)** bad

**gho daish!** help!

**gho desh volu belkhaloo** aid worker

**ghoolähí** (*adjective*) well; **Suuna ghoolähí kheeta.** I feel better.

**ghöönallin organizatsi** charity

**ghorii(n) küügash/koogash** frostbitten hands/feet

**ghoriina** freezing

**ghort** neck

**ghowgha** noise; **ghowgha ma ye!** keep quiet!

**ghowgha yölu** noisy

**ghowghana** noisy

**ghu** well (of water)

**ghullaq** work; business; matter

**ghum** sand

**Ghumqii** Kumyk

**ghunzhara(n)** slanted

**Ghurban ͨiid** Id al-Adha

**ghutaq** box; drawer

**gid** guide

**gigiyena** hygiene

**gipatit** hepatitis

**göö** mattress

**gol** goal

**goola** elbow; knee

**Gollandkhoi(n)** Dutch

**gor latta** to kneel

**gorchitsa** mustard

**gostinitsa** guesthouse; hotel

**goota** plow

**gotta(n)** (*plural* **gattii(n)**) narrow

**gowr** horse; **gowr i wordi** horse and cart

**gowrahí leelar** horse riding

**gowrash khakhkar** horse racing

**gowza(n)** skillful; skillfully

**granat** grenade

**gravii** gravel

**grazhdanalla** nationality

**grazhdanin** citizen

**grazhdanski** civil; civilian **grazhdanski baq'oonash** civil rights; **grazhdanski t'om** civil war

**grazhdanstvo** (international) nationality

**Grecheski; Grekii(n)** Greek

**gripp** flu

**gruz** cargo; freight

**gubka** sponge

**guu** hill

**güiree** autumn

**gullam** assembly

**gullamyah yolu mettig** seat (in assembly)

**gumanitarni gho desh wola belghalo** aid worker

**gumanitarni gho** humanitarian aid

**Gürzhii(n)** Georgian

**gyenotsid** genocide

# gyerga

**gyerga** nearby; nearly
**gyergar nakh** relatives
**gyergga** right next to; almost; exactly

# H H'

**ha'** yes
**h'ach** plum
**h'ada** to burst
**h'agg** thirsty; **So h'agga wella/yella.** I'm thirsty.
**haa-ha'** no
**h'aiba** cow
**h'ainig** (*singular*) your; yours
**h'akkha** draw
**h'ala** up
**h'al da** to build
**h'alghara** first
**h'al ghatta(n)** to get up
**h'alkha** front; in front of; forwards
**halkha bullu maagha** safety pin
**h'alkhara** first
**h'alkhara küzg** windshield
**h'al ölla(n)** hang (a person)
**h'anna** who to?
**h'aqa** to saw
**h'äqa** pig
**h'aqolg** ankle
**hara** this; **hara yu/wu/du/bu h'uuna** here is/are
**h'aara** could; could
**hara zama** present (time)
**h'aasha** visitor
**h'äshk'a** corn
**h'ätta** avalanche
**hawa'** air
**h'azh ts'a vakhar** haj; pilgrimage (to Mecca)
**h'azha(n)** to taste; to try; to look for; to wait
**h'azho** haji; pilgrim (to Mecca)

**h'ekh** cave
**h'eekha** to teach
**h'ekharkho** teacher
**h'ekharna konsultant** training consultant
**h'eelii** (*plural; singular* **yeett**)) cows
**h'eenyekh** someone
**h'eq'alalla** wisdom
**h'eera** mill
**h'eravälla** insane
**h'eera wodu tsamgar** rabies
**heesha ts'a** guesthouse
**hey!** hey!
**h'iiza war** torture
**h'iiza yar** rape
**h'iizo** to spin
**hintsa** now
**hintstsa** right now
**Hirii(n)** Ossete
**h'o** (*singular*) you; yourself
**hoqa ⁣ᶜüirana** this morning
**hoqa k'irnah'** this week
**hoqa sharah'** this year
**hoquzah'** here
**horbaz** watermelon
**hord** sea
**horda(n) yiist** coast
**h'oshtagh** toilet
**h'ostam** nail
**hotta(n)** to stand; to become
**h'ozha** smell
**h'ozha yan** to stink
**hu** seed
**hu'a 'a** something
**huma lachq'a yara** theft
**huma** thing
**humanash töögurg** dressmaker
**humma 'a** nothing
**humma dats!** it doesn't matter!
**humnash dh'a yaqqar** robbery
**humnash yüttu mettig** laundry service

**hu(n)?** what?
**h'un** forest; wood
**h'uuna hu yeeza?** what do you want?
**hunda?** why?
**hush dh'a deer** sowing
**hush** seeds
**h'üzhar** madrasa
**h'wo** (*singular*) you; yourself
**hwor** each
**hworsh** these
**hwotta(n)** to stand up
**h'yezha(n)** to look for; to glare; to stare

# I

**i** and ; he; she; it; this
**ikra** caviar
**ᶜilla(n)** to lie (down)
**ᶜilma** science
**ᶜilmancha** academic; scientist
**ᶜilmanii(n) akademi** academy of sciences
**imam** imam
**imigratsi** immigration
**Indi** India
**Indusii(n) din** Hinduism
**Indusii(n)** Hindu
**infarkt** heart attack
**infektsi** infection
**Ingals(an)** British; English
**inginer** engineer
**Injiil** Bible
**instrument** tool
**Internet** Internet
**ira(n)** sharp
**irkh qiisadala** to leap
**Irlandi** Ireland
**Irlandii(n)** Irish
**isbäh'alcha** artist
**ishkap** cupboard

**ishkol** school
**ishtta** also; such; like this, like that
**Islam** Islam
**iss** nine
**istrebitel** fighter
**Italianii(n)** Italian
**itt** ten
**itt sho** decade
**itu** iron (for clothing)
**iyeshwa** to defeat
**Iyull** July
**Iyunn** June
**iza** he, she, it; this; **iza hu du?** what's that?

# J

**jaz** jazz
**jyerwo** previously married woman
**jinsesh** jeans

# K  K'  KH

**k'a** grain; wheat; **k'a h'eegar** reaping; struggle
**kabel** cable
**kabinet** cabinet; office
**kad** cup
**k'add wala/yala** tired
**ka detta(n)** to seize
**kagda(n)** to break
**k'ai** white
**kalkulyator** calculator
**k'am dalar** itch
**kamer** inner-tube
**kamiritsa bolu ghirsa** camera equipment
**Kanada** Canada
**Kanadii(n)** Canadian
**kanal** (tv) channel

**k'ant** boy; son
**k'ant: t'e h'iiza k'ant** boyfriend
**kantselyarski (tovarsh dukhka) tüka** stationer's
**kapot** bonnet
**Karachai** Karachai
**karandaash** pencil
**kari ya(n)** to find
**kaarnash** gloves
**karta** map
**kartolg** potato
**kaseta** tape (cassette)
**kash** tomb
**kassa** cashier; ticket office
**kastom** jacket
**katastrofa** disaster
**Kavkaz** Caucasus
**kazino** casino
**kech ya** to prepare
**k'eeda** soft
**k'eeda ᶜa(n)** mild winter
**k'elo** ambush
**k'ezzig** a bit; a little
**k'ezzigakha** less
**k'ezzigakh daaq'a** minority
**k'elh'aara vaqqar** relief aid
**k'elh'ardaala** escape
**k'elkha'ar** ambush
**kechup** ketchup
**keekhat** (piece of) paper; letter
**keema oh'a khu'ush mettag** landing strip
**k'eg** bottom
**kekhata(n) salfetka** napkin
**kellä** new
**keema** airplane; boat
**kemsash** grapes
**ker dooghacha sharah'** next year
**ker dooghacha k'irnah'** next week
**kerla** fresh
**kerla dootsu** stale
**kerla(n)** new

**Kersta(n)** Christian; Orthodox
**Kersta(n) dina** Christianity
**kert** fence
**keshnash** cemetery
**k'ezzig** less
**-kh** -er
**kha'am** sign
**kha'a(n)** to sit; to know (something)
**kha'a dala** to feel
**kha'a yala (hozha)** to smell
**khabar** news; talk; nonsense
**khädda: Linii dh'a khädda.** The lines have been cut.
**khado** to chop down
**khala** difficult
**khalkhar** dancing
**khan** time; age
**h'aqi(n) zhizhig** pork
**kharts** false
**khartsa: H'o khartsa löö.** You are wrong.
**kharzha; (s'h'a) kharzha** to choose; to vote; to elect
**kharzhamash** election
**khasbesh** garden
**khasstöömash** vegetables
**khattar** question
**khaza** (adjective) nice; (verb) to hear
**khazalla** beauty
**khazna** treasury
**khecha** trousers
**kheeda** cut
**kheedar** plate
**kheetsa akhcha** to change money
**khaza(n)** to hear
**khena hottam** weather
**kheena(n) däᶜakhk** pelvis
**kherkh** saw
**khi** river; water
**khi yist** river bank
**khi t'edaalar** flood

**khi(n) t'iah' lelash yolu miina**
  floating mine
**khiidöq'e** (water) channel
**khila(n)** to be
**khiitsa(n)** replace
**khila zama** past
**khila(n): (ts'hangäh') khila(n)** to
  have
**khi(n) korta** upriver
**khi(n) shisha** water bottle
**khiira stag/zuda** stranger
**khirurg** surgeon
**khlopok** cotton
**kho'** egg; (military) shell
**kholera** cholera
**kholodilnik** fridge
**khorsha** fever
**khotta** mud
**khozyaistvenni tüka** hardware
  store
**khyetsam kyertsa** to change
**kibarchik** brick
**kiicha: So kiicha wu/yu.** I am
  ready.
**kiila** kilogram
**k'ira** week;' **k'ira dälcha** next
  week
**kiira** stomach
**kiira lazar** stomachache
**K'iran de** Sunday
**kilometar** kilometer
**kils; kilsa** church
**kinishka** book
**kinorezhisser** filmmaker
**kinoteatr** cinema
**kirka** pickaxe
**kisa** pocket
**kislorod** oxygen
**kitaab** book
**kiyosk** kiosk
**klinika** clinic
**kniiga** book
**knizhni tüka** bookshop

**k'oo** spicy
**k'oa yotsu burch** sweet pepper
**koch** dress; shirt
**kod** area code
**kofe** coffee
**kog** leg; foot
**kooga p'elg** toe
**kogsaalazash khekhkar** skiing
**kolej** college
**kolonna** convoy; column
**komanda** team
**kombain** combine harvester
**komisionii** commission
**kommunizm** communism
**kompakt disk** cd
**kompakt disk player** cd player
**kompas** compass
**kompensatsi** compensation
**kompütor; kompyutor** computer
**komunist** communist
**konditsiyoner** air conditioning
**konferentsi chöö** conference
  room
**konfeta** candy
**konstitutsi** constitution
**konsulstvo** consulate
**konsultant** consultant
**kontrabandist** smuggler
**kontsentratsionni laager**
  concentration camp
**kontsert** concert
**kontserta(n) zal; kontsertni zal**
  concert hall
**kontuzi** concussion
**konvert** envelope
**konvoi** convoy
**konyak** brandy
**kopi** copy
**kor** window
**k'orshamee** rude
**korabal** boat
**korm** (noun) feed
**kormatalla** ability; profession

**koruptsi** corruption
**kort** head
**kort laza** headache
**kört ghaala** capital city
**körta maidan** main square
**körtnig mil wu?** who is in charge?
**kostüm** suit
**kootam** chicken; hen
**kran** crane; faucet
**Krasni Krest** Red Cross
**kreditni karta; kreditni kartochka** credit card
**kremen** flint
**krizis** crisis
**kseroks** photocopier
**küg** hand
**küg ta<sup>c</sup>o** sign
**küg yazdara** signature
**küüga yina huma** handicraft
**kui** hat
**küiga belghalo** manual worker
**küigalkho** administrator; manager
**küigalkho** leader
**kukhne; kukhni** kitchen
**kupe yolu vagon** sleeping car
**kupeini** business class
**k'ur** smoke
**kura** proud
**kuralla** pride
**küüsa(n)** leafless
**kuuza** carpet
**küzga** mirror
**küzganash** eyeglasses; sunglasses
**kvartira** apartment; headquarters
**kvartira(n) ts'eeno** apartment block
**kvartirii(n) tsa** housing project
**kwoch** shirt
**kwog** leg; foot
**kwort** head
**k'yela** under

# L

**la'a** wish
**la'amalla** independence
**la'amee** independent
**la'amee pachkhalq** independent state
**lach'q'a(n)** hide
**ladoogha(n); ladwogha(n)** listen
**laager tuukha mettig** campsite
**läh'a** snake
**lak** varnish
**lakhka(n)** to chase; to expel
**lam** mountain
**lama** the day after tomorrow
**laama(n) k'aazha** foothills
**laamana(n) h'ätta** avalanche
**laamana(n) mogha** range
**laamasta(n)** traditional
**laame** ladder
**lampa** lamp
**laarame: Iza laarame ghullaq du.** It's important.
**laara(n)** to count
**laatsa(n)** to take; to catch to seize
**laatsar** arrest
**läh'o katookhar** snake bite
**lakhah'** below
**laqa(n)** to sing
**lar loo!** danger!
**larda(n)** defend
**lasta(n)** to shake; to shudder; to rock
**latq'am** complaint
**lata(n)** to stick to; to fight
**latar** struggle
**latoo** to light
**lätsna** about; in connection with
**latta(n)** (noun) earth; field; (verb) to stand
**lattoo** to hold; to keep

**laza** to hurt; **Hara stag laza vina wu.** This person is hurt.
**lazar** disease; illness; pain; **lazar satsosh molkha; lazar teedesh molkha** painkiller
**laza wan** to injure
**lazzina: Nakh laziina quzah'.** There are people injured.
**ledara(n)** sloppy; casual
**legash** throat
**legash lazar** sore throat
**leekha** seek
**leela** to move; to go; to fly
**leelo** to drive
**leqa(n)** high; tall
**lerg** ear
**lergakh ukhkarsh** earrings
**levyi** left-wing
**Lezgin** Lezgi
**lezvesh** razorblade
**lift** elevator
**liicha(n)** to bathe; to go bathing
**liider** leader
**limon** lemon
**lineika** ruler
**linza** lens
**linzash choh' latto rastvor** contact lens solution
**linzash** contact lenses
**litar** liter
**loo** snow; **Loo doogha.** It is snowing.
**loo'aa(n) h'ätta** snowdrift
**logha** low
**Looma(n) Zhütkii** Mountain Jew/Tat
**lor** doctor
**loryisha** nurse
**lowza(n)** to play
**lowzar** play; game
**luulakhwo** (plural **luulakhwoi**) neighbor
**lülla** pipe

**lüra(n)** dangerous
**lwo** snow
**lye$^c$a(n)** to destroy
**lyech'q'a(n)** hide
**lyech'q'a(n)** to hide
**lyega(n)** to fall; to leak
**lyepa(n)** to shine; to twinkle
**lyotchik** pilot

# M

**ma** not; do not
**ma-** just as
**ma$^c$ar; m$^c$ara** hook; fork
**ma$^c$arsh khado tukar** nail-clippers
**mach** (sports) match
**maachash** shoes
**madrasa** madrasa
**mafia** mafia
**maagha** pin; needle; syringe
**magnitni miina** magnetic mine
**magnitofon** tape recorder
**Mai** May
**mä$^c$ig** corner
**maira(n)** brave
**makh** price, check; bill; **makh khiila(n)** to cost
**maakha** pin; needle; syringe
**makhkakh vaqqar** exile
**mäkhza(n)** free of charge
**mala(n)** to drink
**mala huma** (noun) drink
**malkh** sun; **malkh qetta** sunny; **Malkha häzhna de(n) du.** It is sunny.
**malkh ts'a qachar** solstice
**malkhbaali** east
**malkhbuzi** west
**malkhbuzu khan** sunset
**malkhekh lardesh dolu krem** sunscreen

# mä<sup>c</sup>na khiila(n)

mä<sup>c</sup>na khiila(n) to mean
mänga bed
mangal scythe
mar husband
mara nose
maariah' *female* married
maari yaghaz *female* single
maashar peace
mark deutschemark
marka stamp
markha cloud
markha dasta to break a fast; **Sa
  markha du.** I am fasting.
**Markha Dostu <sup>c</sup>iid** Id al-Fitr
markhash yolu cloudy
**Markhii(n) Butta** Ramadan
märsha free; unarmed
märsha vaalar liberation
märsha wooghiil! welcome!
märshoo freedom
**Mart** March
marta breakfast
masa? how many?
mashana(n) tüka dairy
mashen car; machine
mashena(n) doogha wrench
mashena(n) nomer car
  registration
mashena(n) zapchastesh yukhku
  tüka car spares store
masla<sup>c</sup>at peace; truce; cease-fire
masla<sup>c</sup>ata(n) peregovorash
  peace talks
masla<sup>c</sup>at lattosh eskarsh peace-
  keeping troops
masso; massara all together
masswo 'a all
mats: So mats vella/yella. I'm
  hungry.
matsa? when?
mazh beard; mazh yöösha krem
  shaving cream
mäzhdig mosque

mediyator negotiator
medsestra nurse
meekara(n) treacherous
mekhala huma jewelry
mekhanik mechanic
meekhi pins and needles
mel? how much?; **mel geena?**
  how far?; **mel ulläh'?** how
  near?
mellish slow
meloch loose change
mentol menthol
menü menu
meeqa rust
meeqash mustache
merza sweet; tasty
merza huma candy
mesash hair
mesash khaado mettig barber's
metall metal
metar meter
metrika birth certificate
metsa: So metsa wu/yu. I'm
  hungry.
metta instead
mettig place
mettig seat (in assembly)
meza louse
mezhdunarodni international;
  **mezhdunarodni kod**
  international code;
  **mezhdunarodni operator**
  international operator
meezhee limb; meezhee dh'a
  yaqqar amputation; meezhee
  kagyar fracture
michah'? where?; michah'
  wu/yu/bu? where is/are?
**MID** Ministry of Foreign Affairs
miel? how much?
miella 'a some amount
miil mile
mila? (*plural* mülsh) who?

**mikroskop** microscope

**militsi** police

**militsi otdel** police station

**militsiyoner** policeman

**milla 'a** someone; anyone

**milyon** million

**miina** (*noun*) mine; **miina dh'a yaqqar** clear a mine; **miina iila eqqar** to lay mines; **miina t'iah eqqar** hit a mine; **miinash bilgal yookhush detektor** mine detector; **miinash** mines; **miinash zee naz ya** mine disposal

**minara** minaret

**mineralni khi** mineral water

**miinii(n)** (*adjective*) mine

**miinii(n) aare** minefield

**ministar** minister

**ministerstvo** ministry

**Ministerstvo transporta** Ministry of Transport

**Ministerstvo Oboroni** Ministry of Defense

**Ministerstvo Obrazovanya** Ministry of Education

**Ministerstvo Yustitsii** Ministry of Justice

**miiting** (political) demonstration

**miiting daaq'akho** (political) demonstrator

**minot** minute

**Minselkhoz** Ministry of Agriculture

**Minzdrav** Ministry of Health

**mobilni telefon** mobile phone

**mochkhal** jaw

**modem** modem

**moogha** how

**mogshalla** health

**mogush** healthy; well

**mokh** wind

**mookha** how

**mokh bälla** windy

**mokhk beegor** earthquake

**mokhk** country

**molkha** drug; medication; pill

**molkhanash** medication

**molu khi** drinking water

**moment** moment

**monastir** monastery

**mokh bolu** windy

**moosha** partridge

**moozha** yellow

**moqa** penknife

**moqaz** flint

**morozhni** ice cream

**moskal** turkey

**mostagh** enemy

**motor** engine

**motora(n) remenn** fan belt

**mototsikal** motorbike

**mott** language; tongue

**motta biitsa** to speak a language

**moza** (*noun*) fly

**muq'a dakhka** rat

**mukhkha 'a** somehow

**mülkha?** which?, what kind?

**mülkhkha 'a** some kind

**mülsh?** (*plural*) who?

**muq'a: Linii muq'a yats.** The line is busy.

**muq'a dakhka** rat

**muq'a khan** holiday; leisure time

**muq'ana** at least

**müst** sour; **müsta h'ach** sour plum

**müta<sup>c</sup>eelim** (religious school) pupil

**muzei** museum; art gallery;

**muzika** music

**MVD** Ministry of Home Affairs

**mwostagh** enemy

**mwott** language; tongue
**myerzalla** sweetness

# N

**nab** sleep; **nab qöötiit molkha** sleeping pills
**nabakhtee** prison
**nab yan** to sleep
**nab yookha** sleepy
**naiyömnik** mercenary
**nakh** (*plural; singular* **stag**) people
**nalog** tax
**nana** mother
**n^cana** rooster; worm
**naaqa** breast; chest
**naaq'ost** colleague; companion
**naqar moza** bee
**närs** cucumber
**nasos** pump
**nauka** science
**n^cäwtsitsig** caterpillar
**nazh** oak
**nefte pererobativayushchi zavod** oil refinery
**nefteprovod** oil pipeline
**neitralnyi** neutral drive
**neeka** swimming
**neeka dan** to swim
**nekhcha** cheese
**Nemtsoi(n)** German
**neena da(n)** *maternal* grandfather
**neena nana** *maternal* grandmother
**neq'** road
**neeq'a(n) karta** road map
**neq'goiturg** guidebook
**nerveni gaz** nerve gas
**nifrit** jade
**niisa** straight; true; **niis(a) dh'a** straight on; **H'o niisa löö.** You are right.
**niisa tsa qeetar/vowshe tsa**

**qeetar** to misunderstand
**niiswoo** justice
**nitsq'** strength
**nizam** law
**nochnoi klub** nightclub
**Noghii(n)** Nogai
**Nokhchii(n)** Chechen; **Nokhchii(n) mott** the Chechen language; **Nokhchii(n) Mokhk** Chechnya; **Nokhchi khalkhar** Chechen folk dancing; **Nokhchi muzik** Chechen folk music
**Nokhchwo** Chechen
**nomer** number; hotel room; **nomera(n) servis** room service
**nosilkash** stretcher
**Novi Zilandi** New Zealand
**novostesh yesha** newscast
**novostin agentstvo** news agency
**Noyabar** November
**nui h'akkha** to sweep
**nul** nought; zero
**nütsaq'ash sa de^ciitar** mouth-to-mouth resuscitation
**nwokh** (*plural* **nazarsh**) jaw; plow
**nwokh daaqqa(n)** to chew; to plow
**Nwokhchi** *see* **Nokhchi**
**Nwokhchwo** Chechen

# O Ö

**oah' ^caana(n)** to spill
**obanash baakha** kiss
**obed** lunch
**obunoi tüka** shoeshop
**ofis** office
**ofis-belghalo** office worker
**ofitser** officer

**ööghaz vakhna** angry
**ogorod** garden
**oh'a** down
**oh'a vizha(n)** to lie down
**oh' tooghar lattar** wrestling
**oila** idea
**oila khila(n)** to intend
**oila yan** to think; to judge
**olla(n)** to hang (something)
**Oktyabar** October
**okupatsi** occupation; **Nokhchi mekhka(n) okupatsi** occupation of Chechnya
**okupatsii(n) eskarsh** occupying forces
**olkhazar** bird
**O.O.N.** United Nations
**opera** opera; opera house
**operator** operator
**operatsi** surgery; operation
**operatsii(n) zal** operating theatre
**oppositsi** opposition
**or** (plural **ornash**) hole
**ooramat** crops; plant
**ooramatash dooghar** planting
**ooramatash leeloo** to grow crops
**Orshot (de)** Monday
**Örsii(n)** Russian
**Örsii(n) Pachkhalq** Russia
**oskolkash** shrapnel
**otkritka** postcard
**otkrivalka** can opener; bottle-opener
**otpusk** holiday
**otvertka** screwdriver
**ovoshnoi tüka** greengrocer
**ow** net
**owlaa** saint
**özda** polite; kind
**ᶜozhalla** death
**ozhereli** necklace

# P P'

**pachka** packet
**pakh** lung
**palatka** tent
**palatkiii(n) h'öqanash** tent pegs
**palto** overcoat
**pamyatnik** monument
**pamyatnik** statue
**papka** file
**parashyut** parachute
**parghatee** comfortable
**parikmakher** hairdresser
**parikmakherski** barber's
**park** park
**parlament** parliament
**parlamenta(n) ghishlo** parliament building
**parti** (political) party
**partizan** guerrilla
**pasazhir** passenger
**pashbuq'** ferret
**pasport** passport; **pasporta(n) nomer** passport number
**pasta** melon
**paastash** socks
**patsiyent** (medical) patient
**pechatni mashen** typewriter
**pedeyator** pediatrician
**peekhash** lungs
**pekarni** bakery
**p'elg** finger
**penitsilin** penicillin
**peredacha** gear
**peredachik** transmitter
**perekröstok** crossroads
**perevodchik** interpreter
**perevorot** coup d'état
**pesh** stove
**perevorot** coup d'état
**P'eerska** Friday
**ph'aagal** rabbit

# ph'ars

**ph'ars** arm; wrist
**ph'id** (*plural* **ph'idarchii**) frog
**ph'or** dinner; supper
**pis** stingy
**p'kha** artery
**pkheenash** veins
**pkhi'** five
**pkhiitta** fifteen
**pkhiittalgha** fifteenth
**plastikovi miina** plastic mine
**plastinka** record
**plastir** bandaid
**plastmass** plastic
**platform** platform
**platskartni** second class
**plita** cooker; stove
**ploschadka** pitch
**plyonka** film
**pochta** mail; post office
**pochta(n) yashka** mail box
**poezd** train
**poezda(n) vogzal** train station
**pogoda** weather
**pokhmeliye** hangover
**politik** politician
**politika** politics
**politolog** political scientist
**politsi** police.
**polla** butterfly
**pomada** lipstick
**pomidor** tomato
**poni** pony
**posadkin talon** boarding pass
**posadochni polosa** landing strip
**pochta** mail; post office
**poshta(n) marka** stamp
**poshtovi yashka** mailbox
**posilka** parcel
**posol** ambassador
**posolstvo** embassy
**post** checkpoint
**povar** cook
**povorotnik** indicator light

**prachechni** laundry
**pravaash** driver's license
**pravitelstvo** government
**pravyi** right-wing
**predpriyati** business; enterprise
**premiyer** premier
**preservativ** condom
**pressa** media
**prezident** president
**prezidenta(n) gvardi** presidential guard
**prikaz dan** to give an order
**primiyer ministar** prime minister
**printer** printer
**problema** problem
**professi** profession
**profsoyuz** trade union
**protest** protest
**protez** artificial limb; prosthesis
**protivopekhotni** anti-personnel
**protivotankovi** anti-vehicle
**proyektor** projector
**püchash** lies
**pudar** powder
**punt** pound
**putevoditel** guidebook

# Q Q'

**qa'a deeq'akh shi'** two-thirds
**Qa'ara** Wednesday
**qacha** diet
**q'ailii** secret
**qaiqa(n)** to call; to summon
**q'akho** coffee; **shura tökhna kofi** coffee with milk
**q'am** people; nation; (soviet) nationality
**q'amel dan** to speak; to talk
**q'aamil dats!** no problem!
**qaana** tomorrow; **qaan ᶜüiran** tomorrow morning; **qaan delq'khan t'iah'** tomorrow

afternoon; **qaana ᶜiicha** the day after tomorrow; **qaan sarah'** tomorrow night

**q'arq'a** vodka

**q'ätta(n)** bitter

**qärzna kartolgash** french fries

**qazh** vote

**qazh tasar** voting

**qazh tasar khartsa daqqar** vote-rigging

**q'eecha pachkhalq** foreign

**q'eecha pachkhalqyer stag/zuda** foreigner

**qeecha pachkhalqe döödu kema** international flight

**qeiqin ve'ana dokladkho** guest speaker

**qeela** mare

**q'eematee** terrible

**q'eena** old

**qeram** danger

**qeramzalla** safety; security

**qeeta** to understand; **So qeeta.** I understand.

**qi'a** grow

**q'ig** crow

**qi humma dats!** that's all!

**q'ilbi** south

**q'ilbasiidi** north

**qin** other

**qiira pkheeghash** pottery

**q'iisam** struggle; dispute

**qi ts'h'a** another; extra

**qo'** three

**qo'alagha daaq'a** one-third

**qo'algha** third

**qo de h'algha** three days before

**q'oilana** closed; shut

**qoitta** thirteen

**q'okhtsal saara** barbed wire

**q'oola** theft

**q'oola dan** to steal

**q'oolam** pen; pencil

**qöölana** cloud

**q'ooma(n) muzik** folk music

**q'ora** deaf

**qossa(n): top qossa(n)** to shoot

**q'u** thief

**Qur'aan** Qur'an

**quuza** three times

**quzah'** here

**quuztq'a** sixty

**quuztq'ee itt** seventy

**quztq'a** sixty

**quztq'ee itt** seventy

**quzzagkhula** this way

**qwo'** three

**qwo'algha** third

**qwossa(n)** to throw; **twop qwossa(n)** to shoot

**qyeh'a(n)** to drag, pull

**qyera(n)** to fear

# R

**radar** radar

**radiyator** radiator

**radiyo** radio; **radiyo peredaacha** radio broadcast; **radiyo stantsi** radio station

**ragbi** rugby

**rak** cancer

**rakeeta** missile

**raketash** missiles

**Rasii** Russia

**raspisani** timetable

**ratsiya** walkie-talkie

**rayon** district; suburb

**reaktsionni** reactionary

**registratsi** check-in

**registratsii(n) sektsi** check-in counter

**reis** flight

**remen** fan belt

**remont** repair

**remont yan** to repair
**reparatsi** reparation
**respublika** republic
**restoran** restaurant
**revolutsi** revolution
**reeza** happy
**reeza vootsush** unhappy
**rezen** rubber
**rok** rock 'n' roll
**roman** novel
**rozetka** plug
**ruchka** pen
**rügzak** backpack
**rul** steering wheel

# S SH

**saa** corner
**saaba** soap
**sada<sup>c</sup>ar** (*noun*) break; rest
**sa daala(n)** to die
**sagal** flea
**sagalmat** insect
**sagalmatash yoi'u molkha** insecticide
**sagatda(n)** worry
**sah't** clock; watch; hour; o'clock; time
**sah't toodesh mettig** watchmaker's
**sai** deer
**sainig** mine (*belonging to me*)
**sakhillar** sunrise
**salat** salad
**saalaz khekhkar** skating
**salfetkash** tissues
**sälnash** ruins
**salon** salon shop
**salti** soldier; troops
**sama waqqar** wake-up call
**samovar** samovar
**sa muq'a daala(n)/daaqqa(n)** to relax

**samuq'nii** funny
**sam walla/yalla** to wake up
**sam waqqa/yaqqa** to wake (someone)
**sarah'** in the evening
**saarg** cable; wire
**saargakh tesna yolu miina** tripwire mine
**satasar** dawn
**satsa(n)** to stop
**satsiita!** stop!
**satto** bend
**Savyet Pachkhalq** Soviet Union
**schötka** hairbrush
**schyot** check; bill
**secretar** secretary
**seeda** star
**segli** fleas
**seif** safe
**selkhan <sup>c</sup>üiran** yesterday morning
**selkhan sarah'** yesterday afternoon
**selkhan(a)** yesterday
**sendvich** sandwich
**Sentyabar** September
**septsisan** septic
**serlo yala** to shine
**servis** service
**sever** north
**Severni Irlandi** Northern Ireland
**s'h'a 'eetsa** to get; to take; to accept
**sha** ice
**s'h'a** to; into; (to) here
**shaa** himself; herself; itself
**sha ban** freeze
**sha boogho dig** ice axe
**shainig** theirs; (*plural*) yours
**shaita(n)** devil
**shakhmatash** chess
**shakhta** (excavated) mine
**shakhtör** miner

**shal dina berash** twins
**s'h'allataya(n)** switch on
**shampun** shampoo
**s'h'aqaachar** arrivals
**s'h'a qoocha de** date of arrival
**sharf** scarf
**shaarikovi ruchka** ballpoint
**shärshuu** sheet
**shäsh** themselves; yourselves
**shatq'a** weasel
**s'h'a ya** to bring
**s'h'a yasta** undo
**s'h'a yella** open
**shchöt** check; bill
**shchötka** brush
**she(n) doolah' dolu** personal
**sheekar** sugar
**shell** cold
**shelvalar** (medical) cold
**shenig** his; hers; its
**sheeq'a** ink
**sheeq'ana basah'** purple
**shi'** two; **shi k'ira** fortnight; **shi
sho dälcha** the year after
next; **shi sho h'algha** the year
before last; **shi yo^c/shi k'ant**
twins
**Shinara** Tuesday
**shi' privod yölu mashen** four-
wheel drive
**shiila** cold; cool; **shiila khi** cold
water
**shiilo** cold; frost
**shiina** (doctor's) splint
**shitta** twelve
**shira** ancient
**shisha** bottle
**shi' vuzhush chöö** double
room
**shlang** hose
**sho** year; **H'a mass sho do?** How
old are you? **Sa . . . sho do.** I
am . . . years old.

**shok** (medical) shock
**sholgha** second; next
**Shoot** Saturday
**Shotlandi** Scotland
**Shotlandii(n)** Scottish
**showztq'a** forty
**showztq'ee itt** fifty
**shoz** twice
**shpiyon** spy
**shtab** headquarters
**shtopor** corkscrew
**shu** you (plural)
**shura** milk
**shüüra** wide
**shurekh yina humanash**
dairy
**shurup** screw
**shwo** year
**sii** soul; spirit
**sideni** seat
**si-di** cd
**sigar** cigar
**sikha** quick
**sikha: So sikha wu/yu.** I'm
in a hurry.
**sikond** second
**siina** blue
**sinagoga** synagogue
**singattamii** worried
**sinq'eeram** party
**sir** enamel
**sirla-ts'ee** pink
**sirnikash** matches
**siisar** yesterday night
**sistema** system
**sizon** season
**skori pomosh** ambulance
**skorost** speed
**skoryi** express
**slovar** dictionary
**snaryad** (military) shell
**so** I
**sok** fruit juice

**som** rouble
**sotsiyalist** socialist
**sotsiyalizm** socialism
**sovyet** council
**sow** more
**sow bagazh** excess baggage
**sowghat** gift; present
**sowghata(n) tüka** souvenir shop
**spalni meshok** sleeping bag
**spets sluzhba** secret police
**spetsiyalist** specialist
**SPID** AIDS
**spiiker** speaker of parliament
**sport** sport
**spravochni** information; information office
**sputnik** satellite
**sputnika(n) telefon** satellite phone
**stadiyon** stadium
**stag** (plural **nakh**) person; man; human being
**stagga 'a** no one
**stag lachqa var** to kidnap
**stag veera** murder
**stagan nitsqa ba** to torture
**staka; stakan** glass; **stakan ᶜaig** teaspoon
**stantsi** station
**statuya** statue
**ste** female
**stega(n)** (adjective) human
**sten-börsha organash** genitals
**stetoskop** stethoscope
**stigal** sky
**stogar** lamp; light bulb; flashlilght
**stokhka** last year
**stol** table; desk
**stolitsa** capital city
**stoomar** the day before yesterday
**stöömash** fruit
**stoyanitka** car park
**strakhovka** insurance;

**meditsinksi strakhovka** medical insurance
**strakhovoi polis** insurance policy
**stsepleni** clutch
**stu** bull
**student** student
**styenga?** where?
**sud** law court
**südkho** judge
**Süilii** Avar
**süiree** evening
**Sülii(n)** Daghestani
**sülkhanash** rosary
**suuna . . . veeza/yeeza/deeza.** I like/want. . .
**sunt** dam
**supermarket** supermarket
**surt** picture; photo; view
**SV ('es-ve')** first class (train)
**svet** electricity
**svetofor** traffic lights
**sviter** sweater
**swo** I; myself
**syel** so much
**syelkhana** yesterday

# T T' TS TS'

**taba(n)** to sneak up
**tabletka** tablet
**taacha** path; footpath
**taa da(n)** to fix
**t'ado** to wet
**t'äh'a** after
**tähh'ar** last
**t'ai** bridge
**taipa** type
**takhan** today
**taksi** taxi
**talkha(n)** to spoil
**t'am** handle
**tamashii** strange

**tammagha** sign

**tamozhni** (*border*) customs

**tamponash** tampons

**tank** tank

**ta<sup>c</sup>o: küg ta<sup>c</sup>o** sign

**tapcha** pistol

**t'argha** wool

**tarkh** rock

**t'ärska** leather

**tasa(n)** to throw

**taatol** stream; canal

**teatar** theatre

**t'eda** wet

**t'e daala** rise

**teema** subject

**teega** to sew

**t'eeh'a** back; behind

**t'eeh'e** bottom

**t'e h'iiza k'ant** boyfriend

**t'e h'iiza yo<sup>c</sup>** girlfriend

**t'eek'al dina tsa** tower

**tekhka** swing

**tekh pasport** car papers

**t'e lata** to attack; to invade

**t'elatar** attack; invasion

**t'e laatsa** undertake

**t'elato** to stick

**telefon** telephone; **telefon tookha(n)/twokha(n)** to telephone; **telefon tsentr** telephone center

**telegrama** telegram

**telekommunikatsi** telecommunications

**teleks** telex

**teleskop** telescope

**televideni** television; **televidenii(n) stantsi** television station

**televizor** television

**t'e lista** to wind

**t'emlo** fighter

**t'eman yeesar** prisoner-of-war

**t'ema(n) yesarii(n) laager** POW camp

**t'ema sud** war tribunal

**t'ema zulm(ash)** war crimes

**termit** termite

**termometar** thermometer

**t'emoo tseera väqqana stag** Displaced Person

**t'e qyeta** to attack

**teshoo** to prove

**t'etowzha** to lean

**t'e yoogh human tüka** clothes shop

**t'e yooghu zama** future

**tezet** funeral

**t'iah' disar** delay

**tidamcho** observer

**tiina** quiet

**tiinalla** silence

**tilla: So tilla.** I am lost.

**tilla(n)** to put (on top)

**t'iirag** string; rope

**tisha** old; **tisha ghala** old city

**tkhainig** our; ours (*exclusive*)

**tkhäsh** ourselves (*exclusive*)

**tkho** we (*exclusive*)

**tkhow** roof

**tkhowsa** tonight

**tkhwo** we (*exclusive*)

**to''al** enough

**to'a** to be enough; **tö'ar du!** that's enough!

**t'om** fight; war; violence

**t'om ba(n)** to wage war

**t'onka** tobacco

**tooghee** valley

**tookha(n)** to hit; to strike

**toola** strawberry

**top** gun; rifle

**top qossa(n)** to shoot

**toqam** landslide

**t'örmag** bag

**tormoz** brake

**tq'a** twenty

**tq'aiyassana** nineteen

**tq'algha** twentieth

**tq'ayesna** nineteen

**tq'ee itt** thirty

**tq'olgha** twentieth

**traktor** tractor

**trankvilizator** tranquilizer

**transformator** transformer; voltage regulator

**trauma** trauma

**tribuna** podium

**troleibus** trolley bus

**tromb** thrombosis

**trubka** pipe

**tsa** not

**ts'a** house; room

**tsa parghat** uncomfortable

**ts'asta** copper

**tsa tö'ush** not enough

**ts'azamash** wild strawberry

**ts'e** fire; name; **H'a ts'e hu yu?** What is your name?

**ts'ee** red

**ts'ee-moozha** orange

**ts'ena** clean; **ts'ena shärshonash** clean sheets

**ts'ena angali** crystal

**ts'eeno** house; building

**tsentr** center

**tseera bäkhna neekha (bezhentsii(n)) laager** refugee camp

**tseera bäkhna nakh** refugees

**ts'eer daaghar** deportation

**tserg** tooth

**tsergakh <sup>c</sup>utturg** toothpick

**tsergash** teeth

**tsergash yokhka** bite

**tsergash yülu pasta** toothpaste

**tsergash yülu schötka** toothbrush

**tsergii(n) lor** dentist

**tserg lazar** toothache

**Ts'ee Zh<sup>c</sup>aara** Red Cross

**ts'h'a'** one

**ts'h'aa 'a** not one, not a

**ts'h'aitta** eleven

**ts'h'ana** some

**ts'h'a lagha** to search (someone); **ts'h'a huma lagha** to search something

**ts'h'a vüzhush chöö** single room

**ts'h'a zhimma** a little bit

**ts'h'algha** first

**ts'h'an aaghorna böödu uuram** one-way street

**ts'ii** blood; **ts'ii dottar** blood transfusion; **ts'iina gruppa** blood group; **ts'ii ekha** bleed

**tsigah'** there

**tsigärkan keekhat** cigarette papers

**tsigärkash** cigarettes

**tsitska** cat

**tskha** once

**ts'oka** skin

**tsomgash/tsomgush** sick; **So tsomgash wu/yu.** I am sick.

**tsul** more; -er **tsul dika** better; **tsul yoorakh** cheaper; **tsul yoqqa** larger; **tsul zhima** smaller

**tualet** toilet; **tualeta(n) keekhat** toilet paper

**tuinash qiisa** to spit

**tüka** shop

**tukar** scissors

**tükha** salt

**t'ulg** stone

**tür** joke

**turbaza** hostel

**turist** tourist

**turista(n) kartochka** tourist card

**turizm** tourism

**Turkoi(n)** Turkish; Turk

**turniket** tourniquet
**tush** mascara
**tuskar** basket
**t'us s'h'a bosturg** bottle-opener
**twokha(n)** to strike
**twop** rifle; gun
**twop qwossa(n)** to shoot
**t'yarsig** leather
**t'ye** on, onto

# u ü

**uchenik** (school) pupil
**udobreni** fertilizer
**uggar** the most; **uggar dika(n)** best
**ᶜüiran** in the morning
**ᶜüiree** morning
**Ukrainii(n)** Ukrainian
**uksus** vinegar
**ula** three days from now
**ulläh'** near
**ullee** near
**univermag** department store
**universitet** university
**untsi** ounce
**urs** knife; **urs britva** razor; **zhim urs** penknife
**üsh** they
**üshal** marsh; swamp
**üsta; üstagh** ram
**üttalgha** tenth
**uuram** street
**uy** plank; board
**üzash** they

# v

**V.I.CH.** H.I.V.
**vagon-restoran** dining car
**vai** we (*inclusive*)

**vai(n) kheenan** modern
**vaktsin: So vaktsina(n) maakha töghna wu/yu.** I have been vaccinated.
**valar** death
**valyuta** currency
**vanni** bathroom
**väsh** ourselves (*inclusive*)
**vasha** brother
**vaaza** vase
**vechchalg** tick (insect)
**veddarg** (*male*) refugee
**veedar** bucket
**vegetarianets** vegetarian
**vella** (*male*) dead
**venericheski tsamgar** venereal disease
**ventilyator** fan
**veer; stag veer** murder; assassination
**vertolyot** helicopter
**veshanig** ours (*inclusive*)
**veto** veto
**video-kaseta** videotape
**video-magnitofon** video (player)
**videyo** video
**vikhlopnoi turb** exhaust
**vilispet** bicycle
**vilka** plug
**vina de(n)** date of birth
**vina mettig** place of birth
**vina: So . . . .-äh' vina wu.** I was born in . . .
**viinarg** murderer
**vino** wine
**vir** donkey
**virus** virus
**viski** whisky
**vistavka** exhibition
**vitse-prezident** vice-president
**viza** visa

**vizha(n)** to lie down
**V.M.S.** navy
**voditel** driver
**vogzal** railway station
**vo(n)** bad; badly
**voqqa(n)** (plural **baaqqii(n)**) *adjective* elder
**vostok** east
**vowkh** hot
**vowshakh** each other
**vowshakh daqqa(n)** to take apart
**vowshash kah'yezha(n)** to look at each other**vowshakh qeetar** meeting
**vowshakh qyeta(n)** to meet
**vowshakh tyega(n)** to sew together
**vowshi** each other
**vozh** other
**vspishka** flash
**vurhiitta; vürhiitta** seventeen
**vüsh** others
**vüzhu gali** sleeping bag
**V.V.S.** airforce
**vwo(n)** bad; badly
**vworh; vworkh** seven
**vzvivchatka** explosives

# W

**washa** brother
**watt** drum
**Wels** Wales
**Welsii(n)** Welsh
**wisna: So wisna wu.** I am a widower.
**woh'a** down
**woila** idea
**workh** seven
**wu** he is; it is
**wunoo shiila ᶜa(n)** severe winter
**wunoo yowkha** very hot

# Y

**ya** or
**ya: s'h'a ya** to bring
**ya'a(n)** to eat
**ya'a huma** food; meal
**ya'a hum ya; ya'a hum kech ya** to prepare food; to cook
**yala: (huma) yala** to feed; to bribe
**yalkh** six
**yalkhiitta** sixteen
**yalsamani** heaven
**yalta h'eeqa** fertile
**yalta tsakhülu** barren
**yaltash** harvest
**Yanvar** January
**Yaponi** Japan
**Yaponii(n)** Japanese
**yaqqa** to conquer
**yard** yard
**yashar** thaw
**yashka** box
**yay** light
**yaaz da(n)** to write
**yazdarkho** writer
**Ye'arin (de)** Thursday
**yeddarg** (female) refugee
**yeekha(n)** to ask
**yeela(n) khola** haystack
**yeekha** long
**yekhk** comb
**yella** (female) dead
**yett(a)** (plural **h'eelii**) cow
**yetta** to beat
**yetta(n) shura** yoghurt
**Yevropa** Europe
**yeza** expensive; heavy
**yi'narg tsa laarlo** indigestion
**yist** shore
**yillana** open
**yis** frost

**yish** song
**yisha** (*plural* **yizharii**) sister
**yisna: So yisna yu.** I am a widow.
**yist** end
**yista(n)** final
**yitana** divorced: (*male*) **Zuda yitana wu so.**/(*female*) **So yitana yu.** I am divorced.
**yo<sup>c</sup>** daughter
**yoghna: Sa mashen yoghna.** My car has broken down.
**yoh'** face
**yoh'; kolbasa** sausage
**yol** hay
**yolush** included
**yoorakh** cheap
**yootsush** excluded
**yoqqa** big; **yoqqa top; yoq top** cannon; **yoqqa tüka** department store
**yowkha** hot
**yowkharsh** cough
**yowkho** heat; heatwave
**yu** she is; it is
**yug** south
**yugh va(n)** to return
**yui?** there: is there?/are there?
**yukh lurg dala** lend
**yukh lurg daqqa** borrow
**yukha** backwards
**yuq'** divider; interval; middle
**yuq'a** in the middle
**yuq'alelarg** negotiator
**yuqq'a** right in the middle
**yurist** lawyer
**yurkha** blanket
**yurt baakham** farming
**yurt** village
**yurta(n) baakham** agriculture
**yustitsiya** justice
**yu tokha** to sting
**yütt'a** narrow

# Z ZH

**-za** without
**zabastovka** strike
**zadnyi skorost** reverse
**zäi** chain
**zakaz dan** to order; to make an order
**zakaznoi poshta** registered mail
**zakuska** snack
**zalozhnik** hostage
**zapad** west
**zapaska** spare tire
**zapiska** message
**zapisnoi knizhka** notebook
**zasedani** session
**zavod** works; factory
**zavtrak** breakfast
**zazhigalka** lighter
**zazhigalka(n) benzin** lighter fluid
**z<sup>c</sup>e** chain
**zerazaq'** lever
**zezag** flower
**zezagash dukhkurg** florist
**zha** flock
**zh<sup>c</sup>ala** dog
**zhannash** kidneys
**zhen zh<sup>c</sup>ala** sheepdog
**zhii** sheep
**zhim** (*plural* **zhannash**) kidney
**zhim/zhima** little; small; young; **zhim kuuza** kilim; **zhim urs** penknife; **zhima kompütor** laptop computer; **zhima t'örmag** handbag; **zhima televizor** portable tv; **zhima yo<sup>c</sup>** young girl
**zhimma: ts'h'a zhimma** a little bit
**zhizhig** meat
**zhizhig dukh mettig** butcher's
**zhizhigan** butcher's

# zhop

**zhop** answer
**zhop dala(n)** to answer
**zh<sup>c</sup>ow** hammer
**zhowhar** pearl
**zhözhakhati** hell
**Zhügtii(n)** Jewish
**Zhügtii(n) dina** Judaism
**zhurnal** magazine
**zhurnalist** journalist
**ziyaart** shrine
**zintak** ant
**znak** sign

**zontik** umbrella
**zoopark** zoo
**zöpar** splint (*for broken limb*)
**zuda** woman; wife; **zuda yaalin** married *male*; **zuda yaalyaz** *male* single
**zud yaal yar** marriage (= *to take a wife*)
**z<sup>c</sup>üüga** wasp
**zulam** crime
**zulamii(n) stag** criminal
**zvukovoi ghirsa** sound equipment

# ENGLISH-CHECHEN
## INGALS-NOKHCHII

# A

**ability** kormatalla
**Abkhaz** Abkhaz
**about** lätsna
**academic** <sup>C</sup>ilmancha
**academy** akademi
**academy of sciences** <sup>C</sup>ilmanii(n) akademi
**accelerator** gaz pedal
**accident** avaari
**accountant** bukhgalter
**adapter** adapter
**address** adres
**administrator** küigalkho
**after** t'äh'a
**afternoon** delq'a khan t'iah'; **in the afternoon** delq'akhan t'iah'; **yesterday afternoon** selkhan sarah'
**age** khan
**agreement** dogovor; **to sign an agreement** dogovor k'el küg ta<sup>C</sup>o
**agriculture** yurta(n) baakham
**agronomist** agronom
**aid worker** gho desh volu belkhaloo; gumanitarni gho desh wola
**aid** belkhi
**AIDS** SPID
**air** hawa'
**air mail** aviya poshta
**airconditioning** konditsiyoner
**air force** V.V.S.
**airplane** keema

**airport** aeroport
**airport tax** aeroporta(n) nalog
**air raid** bombardirovka
**alcohol** alkogol
**alcoholic** alkagolik
**alcoholism** alkagolizm
**alive** diina(n)
**all** derrig 'a; **that's all!** Qi humma dats!
**all** (plural) massuo 'a
**all together** masso/massara
**allergic: I'm allergic to …** Sa …-na alergii yu.
**allergy** allergii
**allow** baq'o yala(n)
**also** ishtta
**ambassador** posol
**ambulance** skori pomosh
**ambush** k'elkha'ar; k'elo
**America** Amerika
**American** Amerikanets; Amerikii(n); Amerikanski
**amputation** meezhee dh'a yaqqar; amputatsi
**ancient** shira
**and** i; a
**anemia** anemia
**anesthetic** anasteziiya
**anesthetist** anastezist
**angry** deera(n); ööghaz vakhna
**animal** diinat
**animal feed** korm
**ankle** h'aqolg
**another** qi ts'h'a
**answer** (noun) zhop; (verb) zhop dala(n)
**ant** zintak

**anti-freeze** antifriz
**anti-personnel** protivopekhotni
**anti-vehicle** protivotankovi
**antibiotic** antibiotiik
**antibiotics** antibiotikash
**antiseptic** chow dh'a yerzosh molkha; antiseptik
**anyone** milla 'a
**apart: to take apart** vowshakhdaaqqa(n)
**apartment** kvartira
**apartment block** kvartira(n) ts'eeno
**apologize: I apologize.** (to a male) Q'in t'eera walalah' suuna./ (to a female) Q'in t'eera yaalalah' suuna.
**appendicitis** apendıtsiit
**apple** <sup>C</sup>azh (plural <sup>C</sup>eezhash)
**April** Aprel
**Arabic** <sup>C</sup>Arbii(n)
**archaeological** arkheologicheski
**architect** arkhitektor
**area** (place) mettig; (region) rayon
**area code** kod
**arm** ph'ars
**Armenian** Ermaloi(n)
**armored car** B.T.R.
**arms dump** gerza(n) sklad
**army** eskar; armi
**arrest** laatsar
**arrivals** s'h'aqaachar
**arrive** daala(n)
**art gallery** galerei; muzei
**artery** p'kha; dega pkha; arteri
**artificial limb** protez
**artillery** artileri
**artist** isbäh'alcha
**ashtray** chimtosurg
**ask** dyekha(n); yeekha(n); dyekhar da(n)
**aspirin** aspirin
**assassination** (of a male) stag veer; (of a female) zuda yeer

**assembly** gullam
**asthmatic** astma
**at least** muq'ana
**athletics** atletika
**atlas** atlas
**attack** (noun) t'elatar; (verb) t'e lata; t'e qyeta
**August** Avgust
**Australia** Avstrali
**Australian** Avstralii
**autonomy** avtonomi
**autumn** güiree
**avalanche** h'ätta; laamana(n) h'ätta
**Avar** Sülii
**axe** dig
**Azeri** Azerbeijanii(n)

# B

**B&W (film)** 'ärzhi-k'ai
**back** (noun) buq'a; (adverb) t'eeh'a
**backache** buq'a lazar/ann
**backpack** rügzak
**backwards** yukha
**bacteria** bakteriya
**bad; badly** vo(n); gho(n)
**bag** t'örmag
**baggage counter** bagazhni sektsi
**bags** t'örmag
**bakery** pekarni; bepig dottu mettig
**balcony** balkon
**Balkar** Balkarii
**ball** bürk
**ballpoint** shaarikovi ruchka
**bandaid** bint; plastir
**bank** bank; **river bank** khi yist
**bank notes** akhcha(n) keekhatash
**bar** bar
**barbed wire** q'okhtsal saara

**barber's** parikmakherski; mesash khaado mettig
**barn** ambar; bozhal
**barren** yalta tsakhülu
**basement** padval
**basket** tuskar
**basketball** basketbol
**bathe** liicha(n)
**bathroom** vanni
**battery** akumulyator
**battery** batarei
**be** wu/yu; khila
**bear** cha (*plural* cherchii)
**beard** mazh
**beat** yetta
**beauty** khazalla
**become** hotta
**bed** mänga
**bee** naqar moza
**beef** bezhana(n) zhizhig
**beetroot** burak
**before** h'alkhaa
**begin** dwolo
**beginning** yuh'/dh'a voolavalar
**behind** t'eh'a
**below** lakhah'
**belt** dökhk
**bend** satto
**best** uggar dika(n)
**better** dikakh
**better** tsul dika; **I feel better.** Suuna ghooliah' kheeta.
**Bible** Injiil
**bicycle** vilispet
**big** doqqa/yoqqa
**bill** makh; schyot; shchöt
**binoculars** binokal
**bird** olkhazar
**birth** ber(a) dar
**birth certificate** metrika
**bit, a bit** k'ezzig; **a little bit** ts'h'a zhimma
**bite** tsergash yokhka

**bitter** q'ätta(n)
**black** ᶜärzha
**black market** chyorni rinok
**blanket** yurkha
**bleed** ts'ii ekha
**blind** bᶜärze
**blizzard** darts
**block** kvartal
**blood** ts'ii
**blood group** ts'iina gruppa
**blood transfusion** ts'ii dottar
**blow** mokh byetta
**blow up** ekkha
**blue** siina
**blues** bluuz
**board** u; uy
**boarding pass** posadkin talon
**boat** keema; korabal
**body** degh
**bomb** bomba
**bombardment** bombardirovka
**bomb disposal** bomba zeenaz ya
**bomber** bombardirovshik
**bone** däᶜakhk
**bonnet** kapot
**book** kinishka; kitaab; kniiga
**bookshop** knizhni tüka
**boot** bagazhnik
**boots** etkash
**border** dooza
**border crossing** doozanal deeh'avaalar
**born: I was born in . . .** So . . .-äh' vina wu.
**borrow** (akhcha) yukh lurg daqqa
**bottle** shisha
**bottle-opener** otkrivalka; t'us s'h'a bosturg
**bottom** bugha; (*of body*) t'eeh'e; (*informal*) k'eg
**box** ghutaq; yashka
**boy** k'ant

**boyfriend** t'e h'iiza k'ant
**bracelet** braslet
**brake** tormoz
**brandy** konyak
**brave** maira(n)
**bread** beepig
**break down: My car has broken down.** Sa mashen yoghna.
**break** (noun) sa da^c^ar; (verb) kagda(n)
**breakfast** marta; zavtrak
**breast** naaqa
**breed** leelwo
**breeding: cattle breeding** bezhnash leelwo
**brick** kibarchik
**bridge** t'ai
**bring** s'h'a ya
**Britain** Angli
**British** Ingals; Anglii(n)
**brooch** broshka
**brother** vasha; washa
**brought** eetsina
**brown** böömasha
**brush** shchötka
**bucket** chiilik; vedar
**Buddhism** Buddizm
**Buddhist** Buddist
**build** h'al da(n)
**building** ghishlo; ts'eeno
**bull** stu
**bullet** d^c^ändarg
**bumper** bamper
**burn** dago; **to get burned** chakhcha(n)
**burst** h'ada
**bus** avtobus
**bus station** avtovogzal
**bus stop** avtobusa(n) ostanovka
**business** ghullaq; biznis
**business class** kupeini
**business enterprise** predpriyati
**businessman** biznismen

**busy: The line is busy.** Linii muq'a yats yu.
**but** amma
**butane canister** gaz balon
**butcher's** zhizhig dukhk mettig; zhizhiga(n)
**butterfly** polla
**buy** eetsa

# C

**cabinet** kabinet
**cable** kabel, saarg
**calculator** kalkulyator
**calf** eesa
**call** qaiqa(n)
**callus** byerch
**camera equipment** kamiritsa bolu ghirsa
**camera** foto aparat
**campsite** laager tuukha mettig
**can** banka
**can opener** otkrivalka
**Canada** Kanada
**Canadian** Kanadii(n)
**canal** tatol
**cancellation** dh'a daqqar
**cancer** rak
**candle** ch'uuram
**candlestick** ch'uuramhottorg
**candy** konfeta, merza huma
**canister: butane canister** gaz balon
**cannon** yoqqa top
**capital city** kört ghaala; stolitsa
**car** mashen
**car papers** tekh pasport
**car park** stoyanitka
**car registration** mashena(n) nomer
**car spares store** mashena(n) zapchastesh yukhku tüka

**cargo** gruz
**carpenter** dechig-ph'ar
**carpet** kuuza
**carton** blok
**cashier** kassa
**casino** kazino
**cask** cherma
**castle** ghaala
**casual** ledara(n)
**cat** tsitska
**catch** laatsa(n)
**caterpillar** nᶜâwtsitsig
**cattle** däh'nii
**Caucasus** Kavkaz
**cause** dan
**cave** h'ekh
**caviar** ikra
**cd player** kompakt disk player
**cd** si-di; kompakt disk
**ceasefire** *see* **truce**
**cellar** padval
**cemetery** keshnash
**center** tsentr
**century** beᶜ sho; bᶜe sho
**chain** zäi; zᶜe
**chair** ghant
**change** khyetsam kyertsa
**change money** kheetsa akhcha
**channel** (water) khiidöq'e; (tv) kanal
**charge: Who is in charge?**
  Körtnig mil wu?
**charity** (*the act*) sagha/saq'a;
  (*organization*) ghöönallin
  organizatsi
**chase** laakhka(n)
**cheap** dai(n); yoorakh
**cheaper** tsul yoorakh
**Chechen** (*person*) Nokhcho;
  (*adjective*) Nokhchii(n);
  (*language*) Nokhchii(n) mott
**Chechnya** Nokhchii(n) Mokhk
**check** makh; shchöt
**check-in** registratsi

**check-in counter** registratsii(n)
  sektsi
**checkpoint** post
**cheese** nekhcha
**chess** shakhmatash
**chest** naaqa
**chew, chew cud** nwokh daaqqa(n)
**chewing gum** seeghaz
**chicken** kootam
**child** beer
**children** beerash
**chin** ch'enga
**cholera** kholera
**choose** (s'h'a) kharzha
**chop down** khadoo
**Christian** Kersta(n)
**Christianity** Kersta(n) dina
**church** kils
**cigar** sigar
**cigarettes** tsigärkash
**cigarette papers** tsigärka(n)
  keekhat
**cinema** kinoteatr
**Circassian** Chergazii
**citizen** grazhdanin
**city center** ghalii(n) yuqqa
**city-map** ghaalin karta
**civilian** grazhdanski
**civil rights** grazhdanski
  baq'oonash
**civil war** grazhdanski t'om
**clean** ts'ena
**clear a mine** miina dh'a yaqqar
**clear land** ts'an dan
**clinic** bolnitsa; klinika
**clock** sah't
**close** dᶜaq'owla
**closed** q'oilana, zakrito
**clothes shop** t'e yoogh huma(n)
  tüka
**cloud** markha; qöölana
**cloudy** markhash yolu
**clutch** stsepleni

**coal mine** shakhta
**coast** horda(n) yiist
**coat** pal'to
**cockroach** chh'awrig
**code** kod; **area code** kod
**coffee** q'akho; kofe
**coffee with milk** shura tökhna
  kofi
**coins** akhcha
**cold** (*noun*) shiilo; shell;
  (*adjective*) shiila(; *medical*)
  shelvalar
**cold water** shiila khi
**colleague** naaq'ost
**college** kollej
**college** kolej
**color** bos
**color film** bos bolu plyonka
**colorless** besa(n)
**comb** yekhk
**combine harvester** kombain
**come** (s'h'a) leela
**come in!** chööh'a waala/yaala!
**comfortable** parghatee
**commission** komisionii; (*financial*)
  akhcha khötsurg lush bolu makh
**communism** kommunizm
**communist** komunist
**companion** naaq'ost
**compass** kompas
**complaint** lat'q'am
**compensation** kompensatsi
**computer** kompyutor
**concentration camp**
  kontsentratsioni laager
**concert hall** kontserta(n) zal;
  kontsertni zal
**concert** kontsert
**concussion** kontuzi
**condom** preservativ
**conference room** konferentsi chöö
**connection: in connection with**
  lätsna

**conquer** yaqqa
**constipation** choo yuq'a
**constitution** konstitutsi
**consulate** konsulstvo
**consultant** konsultant
**contact lens solution** linzash
  choh' latto rastvor
**contact lenses** linzash
**contain: to be contained**
  daakhka(n)
**convoy** konvoi; kolonna
**cook** (*noun*) povar; (*verb*) ya'a hum
  ya
**cooker** plita
**cool** shiila
**copper** ts'asta
**copse** bölak
**copy** kopi
**cork** (*stopper*) t'us; prabka
**corkscrew** shtopor
**corn** h'äshk'a
**corner** mä$^c$ig; saa
**corruption** koruptsi
**cost** makh khiila; deekha
**cotton wool** bamba; khlopok
**cough** yowkharsh
**council** sovyet
**count** laara(n)
**country** mokhk
**coup d'état** perevorot
**cow** yiett (**pl** h'eelii); h'aiba
**crane** kran
**credit card** kreditni karta/
  kartochka
**crime** zulam
**criminal** zulamii(n) stag
**crisis** krizis
**crops** ooramat
**crossroads** perekröstok; galmorze
**crow** q'ig
**cruel** sii dotush q'iiz
**cry** dyelkha(n)
**crybaby** ch'ee$^c$a

**crystal** ts'ena angali
**cucumber** närs
**cup** kad; chashka
**cupboard** ishkap
**currency** valyuta
**customs** (*at border*) tamozhni
**cut** kheeda; **The lines have been cut.** Linii dh'a khädda.

# D

**Daghestani** Sülii(n)
**dairy** shurekh iina humanash; mashana(n) tüka
**dam** sunt
**dancing** khalkhar
**danger** qeram; **danger!** Lar loo!
**dangerous** lüra(n)
**Danish** Datkhoi(n)
**dark** <sup>c</sup>ärzha
**dark** (*noun*) boda
**date** de; **date of arrival** s'h'a qoocha de; **date of birth** vina den; **date of departure** dh'a wööda de; **What is the date today?** Takhana hu de du?
**daughter** yo<sup>c</sup>
**dawn** satasar
**day** den; (*24 hours*) dei büüsi; **the day before yesterday** stoomar; **four days before** di' de h'algha; **three days before** qo de h'algha
**daytime** de
**dead** vella/yella
**deaf** q'ora
**death** dalar; <sup>c</sup>ozhalla; deer
**debt** bekhka; deeqar
**decade** itt sho
**December** Dekabar
**deep: How deep is it?** Iza mel k'orga du?

**deer** sai
**defeat** iyeshwa
**defend** larda(n)
**delay** t'iah' disar
**democracy** demokrati
**democratic** demoktii(n)
**demonstration** (*political*) demonstratsi; miiting
**demonstrator** (*political*) miiting daaq'akho; demonstrant
**dentist** tsergii(n) lor
**deodorant** dezodorant
**department store** univermag; yoqqa tüka
**departures** dh'adaghar
**deportation** deportatsi; tseera daaghar
**depot** depo
**deprive** daaqqa(n)
**desk** stol
**dessert** desert
**destroy** lye<sup>c</sup>a(n)
**devil** shaita(n)
**diabetic** diabet
**diagnosis** diyagnoz
**dialling code** kod
**diarrhea** choh' lazar
**dictator** diktator
**dictatorship** diktatura
**dictionary** slovarr
**die** sa daala; **He has died.** I vella.
**diesel** diizel
**diet** dieta; (*slimming*) qacha
**difficult** khala
**dig** akhka
**dining car** vagon-restoran
**dinner** ph'or
**diplomat** diplomat
**diplomatic ties** diplomatii(n) yuq'amettigash
**direct: Can I dial direct?** Operator vootsush telefon tookha lur yui sööga?

**dirty** böögha; büökha(n); ts'ena
**disaster** bookham; katastrofa;
 **natural disaster** <sup>c</sup>aalama(n)
 bookham
**disco** diskoteka
**discussion** diitsar dillar
**disease** lazar
**disk jockey** disk-jokei
**Displaced Person** t'emoo tseera
 väqqana stag
**dispute** q'iisam
**distant** gennara(n)
**district** rayon
**divider** yuq'
**divorced: I am divorced.** *male*
 Zuda yitana wu so./ *female* So
 yitana yu.
**dizzy: I feel dizzy.** Suuna bh'aagor
 hiiza.
**do** dan; **do not** ma
**doctor** lor
**documentary** dokumentalni
**dog** zh<sup>c</sup>ala
**dollar** dollar
**donkey** vir
**doorlock** doogha
**double bed** boqqa mängä
**double room** shi' vuzhush chöö
**down** oh'a; woh'a
**drag** qieh'a(n)
**drain** daassuo
**draw** h'akkha; dilla
**drawer** ghutaq
**dream** gha(n)
**dress** (*noun*) koch; (*verb*)
 duukha(n)
**dressmaker** humanash töögurg
**drill** drel
**drink** (*noun*) mala huma; (*verb*)
 mala(n)
**drinking water** molu khi
**drive** leelo
**driver** voditel

**driver's license** pravaash
**drug** molkha
**drum** watt
**drunk** vöögha(n)
**duck** badd
**Dutch** Gollandkhoi(n)
**dwell** daakha(n)

# E

**e-mail** e-mail; elektroni pochta
**each** hwor
**each other** vowshakh; vowshi
**eagle** ärzu
**ear** lerg
**earrings** lergakh ukhkarsh
**earth** latta
**earthquake** mokhk beegor
**east** malkhbaali; vostok
**easy** aatta(n); ätta
**eat** huma ya'a(n)
**economist** ekonomist
**egg** kho'
**eight** barkh
**eighteen** baarhiitta; berhiitta
**eighty** dööztq'a
**elbow** goola
**elder** (*adjective*) voqqa(n) (*plural*
 baaqqii(n) )
**elect** kharzha
**election** kharzhamash
**electrical goods store**
 elekrotovarsh dukhka tüka
**electricity** svet; elektrichestvo
**elevator** lift
**eleven** ch'aitta; ts'h'aitta
**embassy** posolstvo
**emergency** avari
**emergency exit** avariini
 aaradovliila
**empty** deesa(n)
**enamel** emall; sir

**end** yist; cheqq daalar
**enemy** mostagh; mwostagh
**engine** motor
**engineer** inginer
**England** Angli
**English** Ingals(an); Anglii(n)
**enough** to''al; **to be enough** to'a;
 **(that's) enough!** tö'ar du!
**enter** daala(n)
**entrance** chughoila
**envelope** konvert
**epidemic** epidemi
**epileptic** epilepsi
**equipment** ghirs
**-er** -kh; tsul
**eraser** rezen
**escape** k'elh'ardaala(n)
**ethnic cleansing** etnicheski
 chistka
**Europe** Yevropa
**European Union**
**even better** dikkakh
**evening** süiree
**evening: in the evening** sarah'
**execute** see **murder**
**execution** see **murder**
**excellent** bashkha(n)
**excess baggage** sow bagazh
**exchange** akhcha khiitsar
**excluded** dootsush/yootsush
**excuse me** bekhk ma billalah'
**exhaust** vikhlopnoi turb
**exhibition** vistavka
**exile** makhkakh vaqqar
**exit** aaradovliila
**expel** lakhka(n)
**expensive** deza/yeza
**explode** daat'a(n); ekkha
**explosion** eqqar
**explosives** vzvivchatka
**express** skoryi
**extend** daarzha(n)
**extended** därzhna

**extension** dopolnitelni nomer
**extra** qi ts'h'a
**eye** b$^c$årg
**eyesight** b$^c$är sa

# F

**face** yoh'
**factory** fabrika; zavod
**failure** ätto tsa khilar
**fall** liega(n)
**fall** lyega(n)
**fallowland** aakhar-latta
**false** kharts
**family** dözal
**fan belt** remen; motora(n)
 remen
**fan** ventilyator
**far; far away** geena; geenah'
**farm** ferma; baakham
**farmer** aakharkho; fermer
**farming** yurt baakham
**fast: I am fasting.** Sa markha du.;
 **to break a fast** markha dasta
**fat** derstana; **to get fat** darsta(n)
**father** da; dan
**faucet** kran
**fax** faks
**fear** qiera(n)
**February** Fevral
**feed** (noun) doq'ar; korm; (verb)
 huma yala
**feel** kha'a dala(n)
**female** ste
**fence** kyert
**ferret** pashbuq'
**ferry** buram
**fertile** yalta h'eeqa
**fertilizer** udobreni
**feud** dow
**fever** daagar; khorsha
**field** aaree; latta

**fifteen** pkhiitta

**fifteenth** pkhiittalgha

**fifty** showztq'ee itt

**fight** (*noun*) t'om; (*verb*) lata

**fighter** istrebitel; t'emlo

**file** papka

**fill** duza(n)

**film** plyonka

**film maker** kinorezhisser

**filtered** filter yolu tsigärkash

**filterless** filter yotsush tsigärkash

**final** yista(n)

**find** kari ya(n)

**fine** dika(n)

**finger** p'elg

**fire** ts'e

**firewood** daago dechig

**first** döh'h'ar; ts'h'algha; h'alghara

**first class** SV ( 'es-ve' – *on trains*)

**fish** ch$^C$ara

**fishing** ch$^C$eeri liitsa

**five** pkhi'

**fix** taa da(n)

**flash** vspishka

**flashlight** stogar; fonarik

**flea** sagal

**fleas** segli

**flee** dada(n)

**flight** reis

**flint** kremenn; moqaz

**floating mine** khi(n) t'iah' lelash yolu miina

**flock** zha

**flood** khi t'edaalar

**floor** (*ground*) ts'eenq'a; (*of building*) etazh

**florist** zezagash dukhkurg

**flour** dama

**flower** zezag

**flu** gripp

**fly** (*noun*) moza; (*verb*) leela

**fog** dokhk

**foggy** dokhk dolush

**folk dancing** nokhchi khalkhar

**folk music** nokhchi muzik; q'ooma(n) muzik

**food** ya'a huma

**fool** chh'woch

**foot** kog; (*measurement*) fut

**foothills** lama(n) k'aazha

**foothpath** tacha

**forbid** bekhkam ba(n)

**foreign** q'eecha pachkhalq

**foreigner** q'eecha pachkhalqyer stag/zuda

**forest** h'un

**forget** dits da(n); yits yala(n)

**fork** m$^C$ara

**fort** ghaala

**fortnight** shi k'ira

**forty** showztq'a

**forwards** h'alkha

**four** di'

**four-wheel drive** shi' privod yölu mashen

**fourteen** deitta

**fourth** dö'algha

**fracture** meezhee kagyar

**franc** frank

**free** märsha

**free of charge** mäkhza(n)

**freedom** märshoo

**freeze** sha ban

**freezing** ghoriina

**freight** gruz

**French** Frantsuzii(n)

**french fries** qärzna kartolgash

**fresh** kerla

**Friday** P'eerska

**fridge** kholodilnik

**friend** dottagh; dwottagh

**frog** ph'id (*plural* ph'idarchii)

**front; in front (of)** h'alkha

**frost** shiilo

**frostbite** dah'a dar
**frostbitten hands/feet** ghorii(n)
  küügash/koogash
**fruit** stöömash
**fruit juice** sok
**fuel** benzin; benzin öösha
**fuel dump** benzina(n) sklad
**full: The room is full.** Chöö
  yüzna yu.
**full moon** butt buzar
**full up: I am full up!** So
  vüzna/yüzna.
**funeral** tezet
**funny** samuq'nii
**future** t'e yooghu zama

# G

**gallon** gallon
**game** lowzar; (sports) mach
**gangrene** gangrena
**gangster** gangster/bandit
**garden** khasbesh; ogorod
**garrison** garinzon
**gas** benzin
**gas pipeline** gazoprovod
**gear** peredacha
**genitals** sten-börsha organash
**genocide** genotsid
**Georgian** Gürzhii(n)
**German** Nemtsoi(n)
**germs** bakteresh
**get** s'h'a eetsa; daqqa
**get up** h'al ghatta(n)
**giant** dᶜüüt'a
**gift** sowghat
**girl** zhima yoᶜ
**girlfriend** t'e h'iiza yoᶜ
**give birth** beera dara(n)
**give** dala(n)
**glass** staka(n)

**glasses, eyeglasses** küzganash
**gloves** kaarnash
**go** (dh'a) leela
**go away!** dh'a waalah' quzar!
**go out** aara daala(n)
**goal** gol
**goat** gaaza
**God** Deela
**gold** deshi
**good** dika(nig)
**goodbye** ᶜa dika yöila
**goose** ghaz
**government** pravitelstvo
**grain** k'a
**gram** garam
**grandfather** *paternal* de(n) da(n);
  *maternal* neena da(n)
**grandmother** *paternal* de(n)
  nana; *maternal* neena nana
**grapes** kemsash
**grass** buts
**grateful: I am grateful.** As
  barkalla booghu.
**grave** baarz
**gravel** gravii öösha.
**Greek** Grecheski; Grekii(n)
**green** bätstsara(n)
**greengrocer** ovoshnoi tüka
**grenade** granat
**grind** ah'a
**ground** latta
**grow** qi'a; **grow crops** ooramatash
  leeloo; **grow up** doqqa khiila
**Grozny** Ghaala
**guerrilla** partizan
**guest speaker** qeiqin ve'ana
  dokladkho
**guesthouse** gostinitsa; heesha
  ts'a
**guide** (*noun*) gid; (*verb*) diiga
**guidebook** putevoditel;
  neq'goiturg

# gum

gum, chewing gum seeghaz
gun top; yoq top
gynecologist genekolog

# H

hair mesash
hairbrush schötka
hairdresser parikmakher
hairdryer fen
haj h'azh ts'a vakhar
hajji h'azho
half akh
hammer zh<sup>c</sup>ow
hand küg
handbag zhima t'örmag
handicraft küüga yina huma
handle t'am
hang (something) olla(n); (a
    person) h'al ölla(n) veera
hangover pokhmeliye
happy reeza
hard ch'oogha
hardware store khozyaistveni
    tüka
harvest yaltash
hat kui
have (ts'hangäh') khila(n)
hay yol
haystack yeela(n) khola
he i; iza
head kort
headache kort laza
headquarters shtab; kvartira
health mogshalla
healthy mogush
hear khaza
heart dog; heart attack infarkt;
    heart condition dog ghiila
    khilar
heat yowkhoo
heating coil elektrobigudi

heatwave yowkho
heaven yalsamani
heavy yeza
helicopter vertolyot
hell zhözhakhati
hello as-salaamu <sup>c</sup>alaikum
help! gho daish!
hepatitis gipatit
her shenig
herd bazha
here quzah'; hoquzah'; here
    is/are hara yu/wu/du/bu
    h'uuna
hers shenig
herself shaa
hey! hey!
hide lach'q'a(n); lyech'q'a(n)
high leqa(n)
hill guu
himself shaa
Hindu Indusii(n)
Hinduism Indusii(n) dina
his shenig
hit tookha; to hit a mine miina
    t'iah' eqqar
H.I.V. V.I.CH.
hoarfrost yis
hold lattoo
hole or
holiday müq'a khan; otpusk
hook m<sup>c</sup>ara
horse gowra; horse and cart
    gowr i wordi; horse racing
    gowrash khakhkar; horse-
    riding gowrah' leelar
hose shlang
hospital bolnitsa; bolnitsi
hostage zalozhnik
hostel turbaza
hot dowkha/yowkha;
    dowgha/yowgha; hot water
    dowgha khi; hot water dowgha
    khi; very hot huno yowkha

**hotel** gostinitsa

**hour** sah't

**house** ts'a; ts'eeno

**housing project** kvartirii(n) tsa

**how** mookha; moogha; **how far?**
mel geena?; **how many?** masa?;
**how much?** mel?; myel?; **how
near?** mel ullāh'?;

**human** (*noun*) adam; stag;
(*adjective*) adami(n); stega(n)

**human rights** adami(n) baq'oonash

**humanitarian** gumanitarni

**humanitarian aid** gumanitarni
gho

**hundred** bᶜee

**hungry** mats; **I'm hungry.** So
metsa wu/yu. *or* So mats
vella/yella.

**hurry: I'm in a hurry.** So sikha
wu/yu.

**hurt** laza; **This person is hurt.**
Hara stag laza vina wu.

**husband** mar

**hygiene** gegeyena; gigiyena

# I

**I** so; swo

**ice** sha

**ice axe** sha boogho dig

**ice cream** morozhni

**id** ᶜiid; **Id al-Adha** Ghurban ᶜiid;
**Id al-Fitr** Markha Dostu ᶜiid

**idea** oila

**identification** dokument

**I.D.P.** *see* **Displaced Person**

**ill: I am ill.** So tsomgash wu/yu.

**illegitimate child** bᶜizh

**imam** imam

**immigration** imigratsi

**important: It's important.** Iza
laarame ghullaq du.

**in** chu

**included** dolush/yolush

**independence** la'amalla

**independent** la'amee;
**independent state** la'amee
pachkhalq

**India** Indi

**indicator light** povorotnik

**indigestion** yi'narg tsa laarlo

**infection** infektsi

**influenza** gripp

**information** spravochni;
**information office** spravochni

**Ingush** Ghalghai

**injure** laza wan

**injured: There are people
injured.** Nakh laziina quzah'.

**ink** sheeq'a

**inner-tube** kamer

**innocent** bekhkaza(n)

**insane** h'eravälla

**insect** sagalmat

**insecticide** sagalmatash yoi'u
molkha

**instead** metta

**insurance policy** strakhovoi polis

**insurance: I have medical
insurance.** Söögah' meditsinksi
trakhovka yu.

**insured: My possessions are
insured.** Sa humnash
strakhovka yollush yu.

**intend** oila khila(n)

**interior** chöö

**internal flight** chöh'aara
kema/reis

**international** mezhdunarodni;
**international code**
mezhdunarodni kod;
**international flight** qeecha
pachkhalqe döödu kema;
**international operator**
mezhdunarodni operator

**Internet** Internet
**interpreter** perevodchik
**interval** yuq'
**into** chu
**invasion** t'elatar
**Ireland** Irlandi
**Irish** Irlandii(n)
**iron** echig; (*for clothing*) itu
**Islam** Islam; Busurba dina
**it** i; iza
**Italian** Italianii(n)
**itch** k'am dalar
**its** shenig
**itself** shaa

# J

**jack** domkrat
**jacket** kastom
**jade** nifrit
**January** Yanvar
**Japanese** Yaponii(n)
**jaw** mochkhal; nwokh
**jazz** jaz
**jeans** jinsesh
**jewelry** mekhala huma
**Jewish** Zhügtii(n)
**joke** tür
**journalist** zhurnalist
**Judaism** Zhügtii(n) dina
**judge** südkho
**July** Iyull
**jump start: Can you jump start the car?** Tettana lator yari ash mashen?
**June** Iyunn
**just as** ma-
**justice** niiswoo; yustitsiya

# K

**Kabardian** Gheebartoi

**Kalmuk** Ghalmaqii
**Karachai** Karachai
**keep** lattoo
**ketchup** kechup
**kettle** chaink
**key** doogha
**key** doogha
**kidnap** stag lachqa var
**kidney** zhim
**kidneys** zhannash
**kilim** zhim kuuza
**kill** *see* **murder**
**killer** nakh boi'u stag/nakh boi'u zuda
**kilogram** kiila
**kilometer** kilometar
**kind** (*noun*) taip; **what kind?** mülkha?; (*adjective*) özda
**kiosk** kiyosk
**kiss** obanash baakha
**kitchen** kukhne; kukhni
**knee** goola
**kneel** gor latta
**knife** urs
**know** (*someone*) dowza(n); (*something*) kha'a(n)
**Koran** Qur'aan
**Kumyk** Ghumqii

# L

**ladder** laame
**lake** <sup>C</sup>aam (*plural* <sup>C</sup>āmnash)
**lamb** <sup>C</sup>aakhar
**lamp** lampa; chirq; stogar
**landing strip** posadochni polosa/ keema oh'a khu'ush mettag
**landslide** toqam
**language** mott; mwott
**laptop computer** zhima kompütor
**larger** tsul yoqqa

**last** täh'h'ar
**laundry** prachechni
**laundry service** humnash yüttu mettig
**law** nizam; **law court** sud
**lawyer** yurist; advokat
**lay** dilla; **to lay mines** miina yilla
**lead** diga
**leader** bächcha; küigalkho; liider
**leafless** küüsa(n)
**leak** liega(n)
**lean** t'etowzha
**leap** (irkh) qiisadala
**learn** <sup>C</sup>aama(n)
**leather** t'ärska
**leave** dita(n)
**left** ärroo; **left-hand** ärroo aagho
**left-wing** ärrooh'ara; levyi
**leg** kog; kwog
**lemon** limon
**lend** (akhcha) yukh lurg dala
**lens** linza
**less** k'ezzig; k'ezzigakha
**let** baq'o yala
**letter** keekhat
**level** doqalla
**lever** zerazaq'
**Lezgi** Lezgin
**liberation** märsha vaalar
**library** (noun) biblyoteka; (adjective) biblyotechni
**lie** (to lie down) vizha(n); <sup>C</sup>illa(n) (to tell a lie) äshpash bitta(n)
**lies** äshpash; püchash
**life** daakhar
**lift** (noun) lift; (verb) h'ala 'ai'a(n)
**light** (noun) daala; (adjective of weight) dai(n); (verb) latoo
**light bulb** stogar
**light meter** eksponometr
**lighter** zazhigalka; **lighter fluid** zazhigalka(n) benzin

**like** dyeza(n); **I like. . .** Suuna . . . veeza/yeeza/deeza.; **like this, like that** ishtta
**limb** meezhee
**lip** balda
**lipstick** pomada
**listen** ladoogha(n); ladwogha(n)
**liter** litar
**little** zhima; **a little** k'ezzig; **a little bit** ts'h'a zhimma
**live** daakha(n)
**liver** do<sup>C</sup>ah'
**lizard** mölq'a
**local** electrichka
**located: to be located** daakhka(n)
**long** yeekha
**look; look for** h'azha(n)
**loose change** meloch
**lose** dai'a(n)/yai'a(n)
**lost: I am lost.** So tilla.
**lot, a lot** duqa
**louse** meza
**love** dyeza(n)
**low** logha
**lower** bukhara(n)
**lunch** delq'a(n) yu'urg; obed
**lung** pakh
**lungs** peekhash

# M

**machine gun** avtomat
**machine** mashen
**madrasa** h'üzhar; madrasa
**mafia** mafia
**magazine** zhurnal
**magnetic** magnitni miina
**mail box** pochta(n) yashka
**mail** poshta
**mailbox** poshtovi yashka
**main square** ghalii(n) yuqqa; körta maidan

**majority** duqakha derg
**make** dan
**male** börsha
**man** stag
**manager** administrator; direktor; küigalkho
**manual worker** küiga belghalo
**many** duqa; **too many** duqa-duqa
**map** karta
**March** Mart
**mare** qeela
**marital status** dözal khilar
**mark** mark
**market** baazar
**marriage** zud yaal yar
**married** *male* zuda yaalin; *female* maariah'
**marsh** üshal
**mascara** tush
**match** (*sports*) mach
**matches** sirnikash
**matter** ghullaq; **It doesn't matter.** Humma dats.
**mattress** göö
**May** Mai
**meals** ya'a huma
**mean** mä'na khiila(n)
**meat** zhizhig
**mechanic** mekhanik
**media** pressa
**medication** molkha; molkhanash
**meet** vowshakhqeta(n)
**meeting** vowshakhqeetar
**melon** pasta
**menthol** mentol
**menu** menü
**mercenary** naiyömnik
**message** zapiska
**metal** metall
**meter** metar
**microscope** mikroskop
**middle** yuq'; **in the middle** yuq'a; **right in the middle** yuqq'a

**midnight** büisana yuq'
**midsummer** äkhke yuqqa
**midwife** akusherka
**midwinter** $^C$a(n) yuqqe
**mild: mild winter** k'eeda $^C$a(n)
**mile** miil
**milk** shura
**mill** h'eera
**millet** bworts
**million** milyon
**minaret** minara
**mine** (*excavated*) shakhta; (*explosive*) miina; (*adjective*) miinii(n); **mine detector** miinash bilgal yookhush detektor; **mine disposal** miinash zee naz ya; (*belonging to me*) sainig
**minefield** miinii(n) aare
**miner** shakhtör
**mineral water** mineralni khi
**mines** miinash
**minister** ministar
**ministry** ministerstvo
**Ministry of Agriculture** Minselkhoz
**Ministry of Defense** Ministerstvo Oboroni
**Ministry of Education** Ministerstvo Obrazovanya
**Ministry of Foreign Affairs** M.I.D.
**Ministry of Health** Minzdrav
**Ministry of Home Affairs** M.V.D.
**Ministry of Justice** Ministerstvo Yustitsii
**Ministry of Transport** Ministerstvo transporta
**minority** k'ezzigakh daaq'a
**minute** minot
**mirror** küzga
**missile** rakeeta
**missiles** raketash
**mist** dokhka

**mistake** ghaalat; **to make a mistake** ghaalat daala(n)
**misty** dokhka dolush
**misunderstand** niisa tsa qeetar/vowshe tsa qeetar
**mobile phone** mobilni telefon
**modem** modem
**modern** vai(n) kheenan
**moment** moment
**monastery** monastir
**Monday** Orshot (de)
**money** akhcha
**month** butt
**monument** pamyatnik
**moon** butt; **new moon** butt ts'inbaalar; **full moon** butt buzar
**more** duqa; **more or less** gerga
**morning** <sup>C</sup>üiree; **in the morning** <sup>C</sup>üiran; **this morning** hoqa <sup>C</sup>üirana; **yesterday morning** selkhan <sup>C</sup>üiran
**mosque** mäzhdig
**mosquito** chürk
**most** uggar
**mother** nana
**motorbike** mototsikal
**mountain** lam
**mountain pass** duq'
**Mountain Jew** Looma(n) Zhütkii
**mouse** dakhka
**moustache** meeqash
**mouth** batt; **mouth-to-mouth resuscitation** nütsaq'ash sa de'iitar
**mouthwash** baga khi qorzurg
**move** leela; (to move something) metter yaqqa; **Don't move!** Mettakh ma waalalah'/ yaalalah'!
**much: too much** duqa-duqa
**mud** khotta
**mule** b<sup>C</sup>arza

**murder** (noun) veer; (of a male) stag veer, (of a female) zuda yeer; (verb) den
**murderer** viinarg
**murky** därzhna
**museum** muzei
**music** muzika
**Muslim** Busurban
**mustard** gorchitsa
**mutual aid** belkhi
**myself** swo

# N

**nail** h'ostam
**nail clippers** ma'arsh khado tukar
**name** tse'e; **What is your name?** H'a tse'e hu yu?
**napkin** kekhata(n) salfetka/gata
**narrow** gotta(n) (plural gattii(n))
**nation** q'am
**nationality** grazhdanalla; (international) grazhdanstvo; (soviet) ghaam
**natural disaster** <sup>C</sup>aalama(n) bookham
**navy** VMS
**near** ullee; ulläh'
**nearly** gyerga
**neck** ghort
**necklace** ozhereli
**needle** maakha
**negotiator** yuq'alelarg; mediyator
**neighbor** luulakhuo (plural luulakhuoi)
**nerve gas** nerveni gaz
**net** ow
**neutral drive** neitralnyi
**new** kellä; **new moon** butt ts'inbaalar
**New Year** Kellä Sho
**New Zealand** Novi Zilandi
**news** khabar

**news agency** novostin agentstvo
**newsagent** *see* **stationer's**
**newscast** novostesh yesha
**newspaper** gazet
**next** sholgha; **next week** k'ira dälcha; **right next to** gyergga
**nice** khaza
**night** büisa; büüsa; **yesterday night** siisar
**nightclub** nochnoi klub
**nine** iiss; iss
**nineteen** tq'aiassana; t'q'ayesna
**ninety** dööztq'ee itt; dyezt'q'ee itt
**no** haa-ha'
**no one** stagga 'a
**Nogai** Noghii
**noise** ghowgha
**noon** delq'a khan
**normal** benzin
**north** q'ilbasiidi; sever
**Northern Ireland** Severni Irlandi
**nose** mara
**not** tsa; **do not** ma; **not a/one** ch'aa 'a; **not enough** tsa tö'ush
**notebook** zapisnoi knizhka
**nothing** humma 'a
**nought** nul
**novel** roman
**November** Noyabar
**now** hintsa; **right now** hintstsa; **four days from now** di' de dälcha; **three days from now** ula
**number** nomer
**nurse** loryisha; medsestra
**nut** b<sup>c</sup>aar

# O

**oak** nazh
**obligation** bekhka
**oblique** ghunzhara(n)

**observer** tidamcho
**occipital bone** t'üsk
**occupation of Chechnya** Nokhchi mekhka(n) okupatsi
**occupying forces** okupatsii(n) eskarsh
**October** Oktyabar
**office** kabinet; ofis; **office worker** ofis-belghalo
**officer** ofitser; epsar
**oil** dätta
**oil pipeline** nefteprovod
**oil refinery** nefte pererobativayushchi zavod
**oil can** dätta(n) kanistar
**old** q'eena; tisha; **old city** tisha ghala; **How old are you?** H'a mass sho du? **I am . . . years old.** Sa . . . sho du.
**on** t'ye
**once** tskha
**one** ts'h'a'
**one-way: one-way street** ts'h'a(n) aaghorna böödu uuram; **one-way ticket** dh'a vagha bilet
**onto** t'ye
**open** (*adjective*) dillana/yillana; (*verb*) s'h'a yella
**opera; opera house** opera
**operating theater** operatsii(n) zal
**operation** (*medical*) operatsi
**operator** operator
**opposite** döhh'al
**opposition** oppositsi
**or** ya
**orange** (*fruit*) apelsin; (*color*) ts'ee-moozha
**orchard** besh
**order** (*something*) zakaz da(n); **to give an order** prikaz da(n)
**orphan** da'a nana'a dootsush beera
**Orthodox** Kerstan

**Ossete** Hirii(n)
**other** (*singular*) qin; vozh; (*plural*) vŭsh
**ounce** untsi
**our; ours** (*exclusive*) tkhainig; (*inclusive*) veshanig
**ourselves** (*exclusive*) tkhäsh; (*inclusive*) väsh
**out** aara
**overcoat** palto
**owl** buha
**oxygen** kislorod

# P

**packet** pachka
**padlock** doogha
**pain** lazar
**painkillers** analgin; lazar satsosh molkha
**paint** basar
**pale** besa(n)
**paper** (*substance*) keekhat; (*newspaper*) gazet
**parachute** chetar; parashyut
**parcel** posilka
**park** park
**park: Can I park here?** Quzah' mashen ghottoa megar dui?
**parliament** parlament; **parliament building** parlamenta(n) ghishlo
**part** daaq'a
**partridge** moosha
**party** sinq'eeram; (*political*) parti
**pass: mountain pass** duq'
**passenger** pasazhir
**passport** pasport
**passport number** pasporta(n) nomer
**past** khila zama
**pasta** garznash

**path** taacha
**patient** (*medical*) patsiyent
**pay** akhcha dala
**peace** maashar; masla$^c$at; **peace talks** masla$^c$ata(n) peregovorash; **peace-keeping troops** masla$^c$at lattosh eskarsh
**peach** ghammagha
**peak** boh'
**pearl** zhowhar
**peasant** aakharkhuo
**pediatrician** pedeyator
**pelvis** kheena(n) dä$^c$akhk
**pen** q'oolam; ruchka
**pencil** q'oolam; karandaash
**penicillin** penitsilin
**penknife** moqa; zhim urs
**people** (*singular* **stag**) nakh
**pepper** burch; burts
**perfume** dukhi
**person** stag (*plural* nakh)
**person** stag; adam
**personal** she(n) doolah' dolu
**petrol** benzin
**pharmacy** apteka
**phone** telefon tuokha(n)
**photo** surt
**photocopier** kseroks
**physiotheraphy** fiziyoterapi(ya)
**pickaxe** kirka
**picture** surt
**pig** h'äqa
**pilgrim** (*to Mecca*) h'azho
**pilgrimage** (*to Mecca*) h'azh ts'a vakhar
**pill** molkh; tabletka
**pillow** ghaiba
**pilot** lyotchik
**pin** maagha; **pins and needles** meekhi
**pink** sirla-ts'ee
**pipe** lülla; trubka

**pistol** tapcha
**pitch** ploschadka
**place** mettig
**place of birth** vina mettig
**place** mettig
**plain** aare
**plane** kema
**plank** uy
**plant** ooramat
**planting** (ooramatash) dooghar
**plastic** plastmass; **plastic mine** plastikovi miina
**plate** kheedar
**platform** platform
**play** lowza(n)
**plow** (noun) akhar; (verb) akhka(n)
**plug** rozetka; vilka
**plum** h'ach
**pocket** kisa
**podium** tribuna
**police.** militsii; politsii
**policeman** militsiyoner
**police station** militsi otdel
**polite** özda
**political scientist** politolog
**politician** politik
**politics** politika
**pony** poni
**pork** h'aqin zhizhig
**portable tv** zhima televizor
**portion** daaq'a
**post office** pochta; poshta
**postcard** otkritka
**potato** kartol(g)
**pottery** qiira pkheeghash
**pound** punt
**pour out** <sup>c</sup>aana(n)
**prisoner-of-war** t'ema(n) yesar
**POW camp** t'ema(n) yesarii(n) laager
**powder** pudar
**pregnant: I'm pregnant.** So beerakh yu.

**premier** premiyer
**prepare** kech ya
**present** (noun) sowghat; (verb) hara zama
**president** prezident
**presidential guard** prezidenta(n) gvardi
**pressure: low blood pressure** logha davleni; **high blood pressure** leqa davleni
**price** makh
**pride** kuralla
**prime minister** primiyer ministar
**printer** printer
**prison** nabakhtee
**prisoner-of-war** see POW
**problem** problema; **no problem!** q'aamil dats!
**profession** kormatalla; professi
**projector** proyektor
**prosthesis** protez
**protect** larda(n)
**protection** lardar
**protest** (noun) protest; duh'al khiilar; (verb) dūh'al khiila
**proud** kura
**prove** tesho
**pull** qyeh'a(n)
**pump** nasos
**puncture: I have a puncture.** Sa ch'urg iqqa(n).
**pupil** (school) uchenik; (religious school) mūta<sup>c</sup>eelim
**purple** sheeq'ana basäh'; fyoletovi
**put** dila(n); **to put on** duukha(n); **to put on top** tilla(n)

# Q

**quarter** dö'algha daaq'a; **three quarters** de'a deeq'akh qo'a
**question** khattar

# robbery

**quick** sikha
**quiet** tiina; **keep quiet!** ghowgha
 ma ye!
**quit** *(job)* dh'a vaala *(balkhar)*
**Qur'an** Qur'aan

# R

**rabbit** ph'aagal
**rabies** h'eera woolu tsamgar
**radar** radar
**radiator** radiyator
**radio** radiyo; **radio broadcast**
 radiyo peredaacha; **radio
 station** radiyo stantsi
**railway** ächka neq'; **railway
 station** vogzal
**rain** dogh; dwogh; **It is raining.**
 Dogha doogha.
**ram** üsta; üstagh
**Ramadan** Markhii(n) Butta
**range** laamana(n) mogha
**rape** *(zuda)* h'iiza yar
**rat** muq'a dakhka
**ravine** ch'ozh
**raw** büüda(n)
**razor** urs
**razorblade** lezvesh
**reactionary** reaktsionni
**read** dyesha(n)
**reading** dyeshar
**ready: I am ready.** So kiicha
 wu/yu.
**reaping** k'a h'eegar
**record** plastinka
**Red Cross** Krasni Krest; Ts'ee
 Zh<sup>c</sup>aara
**red** ts'ee
**refugee** bezhenets; **refugee camp**
 boida neekha lager; tseera
 bäkhna neekha bezhentsii(n)
 laager

**refugees** tseera bäkhna nakh;
 bezhentsash
**registered mail** zakaznoi poshta
**regime** <sup>c</sup>eedal
**relative** gergara (stag/zuda)
**relatives** gyergar nakh
**relax** sa muq'a daala(n)/daaqqa(n)
**relief aid** k'elh'aara vaqqar
**religion** din
**remember** daga daa(n)
**repair** *(noun)* remont; *(verb)*
 remont yan
**reparation** reparatsi
**replace** khiitsa
**report** doklad
**republic** respublika
**reservation** bronn
**reserved** zanyato
**rest** sada<sup>c</sup>ar
**restaurant** restoran
**return** *(verb)* yugh va(n); **return
 ticket** dh'ai-s'h'ai vagha
 bilet
**reverse** zadnyi skorost
**revolution** revolutsi
**rice** duga
**ride** dah'a
**rifle** top
**right** ättoo; baq'oo; **right-hand**
 ättoo aagho; **You are right.**
 H'o niisa löö.
**right-wing** ättooh'ara; pravyi
**ring** *(noun)* ch'ug; *(verb)* detta
**riot** bunt
**rise** t'e daala
**river** khi; **river bank** byerd; khi
 yist
**road** neq'; **road map** neeq'a(n)
 karta
**roadblock** blokpost
**rob: I've been robbed.** Söögar
 humnash dh'a yagha.
**robbery** humnash dh'a yaqqar

# rock

**rock** tarkh (*plural* tarkhanash); lasta(n)
**rock 'n' roll** rok
**roof** tkhow
**room** chöö; nomer; ts'a; **room number** chöön nomer; **room service** nomera(n) cervis; gostinitsäh'
**rooster** n<sup>c</sup>ana
**rope** t'iirag
**rosary** sülkhanash
**rouble** som
**rude** k'orshamee
**rugby** ragbi
**ruins** sälnash
**ruler** lineika
**run** dada(n)
**run out: I have run out of gas.** Sa(n) benzin qaachii(n).
**Russia** Rasii; Örsii(n) Pachkhalq
**Russian** Örsii(n); *less polite:* Ghaazaqii(n)
**rust** meeqa

# S

**sack** gali
**sad** ghaighanii
**safe** seif
**safety pin** halkha bullu maagha
**safety** qeramzalla
**saint** ewlyaa'a; **saint's tomb** ewlyaa'a(n) kash
**salad** salat
**salon shop** salon
**salt** tükha
**salty** düra(n)
**samovar** samovar
**sand** ghum
**sandwich** sendvich
**satellite** sputnik

**satellite phone** sputnika(n) telefon
**Saturday** Shoot
**sausage** yoh'; kolbasa
**saw** (*noun*) kherkh; (*verb*) h'aqa
**say** aala(n); diitsa(n)
**scarf** gata; sharf
**school** ishkol
**science** <sup>c</sup>ilma; nauka
**scientist** <sup>c</sup>ilmancha
**scissors** tukar
**scorch: to get scorched** chakhcha(n)
**Scotland** Shotlandi
**Scottish** Shotlandii
**screw** shurup
**screwdriver** otvertka
**scythe** mangal
**sea** hord
**search** (*someone*) ts'h'a lagha; (*something*) ts'h'a huma lagha
**season** sizon
**seat** sideni; (*in assembly*) mettig; gullamyah yolu mettig
**second** (*noun*) sikond; (*adjective*) sholgha.
**second class** platskartni
**secret police** spets sluzhba
**secret** q'ailii
**secretary** secretar
**security** qeramzalla
**see** gan
**seed** hu
**seeds** hush
**seek** leekha
**seize** laatsa(n); ka detta(n)
**sell** dokhka
**send** dah'iita
**September** Sentyabar
**septic** septsisa(n); **The wound is septic.** Choo yakhk yalla.
**serious** ch'oogha
**service** servis

**session** zasedani

**seven** vworkh; workh

**seventeen** vürhiitta

**seventy** quuztq'ee itt

**severe winter** wunooshiila $^C$a(n)

**sew** teega

**shake** lasta(n)

**shampoo** shampun

**share** daaq'a

**sharp** yira(n)

**shaving cream** mazh yöösha krem

**she** i; iza

**sheep** zhii

**sheepdog** zhen zh$^C$ala

**sheet** shärshuu

**shell** snaryad; kho'

**shine** lyepa(n); serlo yala; **to shine a light** fonarr lat ya

**ship** korabal; keema

**shirt** koch

**shock** (*medical*) shok

**shoes** maachash

**shoeshop** obuvnoi tüka

**shoot** top qossa(n); **Don't shoot!** Gerza ma tooghalah'!

**shop** tüka

**shore** yiist

**short** dootsu

**shoulder** belsh

**show** gaita(n)

**shower** dush

**shrapnel** oskolkash

**shrine** ziyaart

**shudder** lasta(n)

**shut** q'oilana

**sick** tsomgush; **I am sick.** So tsomgush wu/yu.

**sign** (*noun*) tammagha; znak, kha'am; (*verb*) küg ta$^C$o; **to sign an agreement** dogovor k'el küg ta$^C$o

**signature** küg yazdara

**silence** tiinalla

**silver** deti

**sing** laqa; ala

**single** *male* zuda yaaliaz; *female* maari yaghaz

**single room** ts'h'a' vüzhush chöö

**sink** (khii(n)) bukha dagha

**sister** yisha (*plural* yizharii)

**sit** kha'a(n)

**six** yalkh

**sixteen** yalkhiitta

**sixty** quuztq'a

**size** baaramäh'

**skating** saalaz khekhkar

**skiing** kogsaalazash khekhkar

**skillfully** gowza(n)

**skilled** gowza(n)

**skin** ts'oka

**sky** stigal

**slanted** ghunzhara(n)

**sleep** (*noun*) nab; (*verb*) nab yan

**sleeping bag** vüzhu gali; spalni meshok

**sleeping car** kupe yolu vagon

**sleeping pills** nab qöötiit molkha

**sleepy** nab yookha

**sleet** deshash dolu loo

**sling** (*medical*) dökhka

**slope** base

**sloppy** ledara(n)

**slow** mellish

**small** zhima

**smaller** tsul zhima

**smell** (*noun*) h'ozha; (*verb*) kha'a yala

**smoke** k'ur

**smuggler** kontrabandist

**snack** zakuska

**snail** etmä$^C$ig

**snake bite** läh'o katookhar

**snake** läh'a

**sneak up** taba(n)

**snow** loo; lwo; **It is snowing.** Loo doogha.

**snowdrift** loo'aa(n) h'ätta
**so much** syel
**soap** saaba
**soccer** futbol
**soccer match** futboli mach
**socialism** sotsiyalizm
**socialist** sotsiyalist
**socks** paastash
**soft** k'eeda
**soldier** salti
**solstice** malkh ts'a qachar
**some** ts'h'ana; **some kind** mülkhkha 'a; **some amount** myella 'a
**somehow** mukhkha 'a
**someone** h'eenyekh; milyekh; milla 'a
**something** hu'a 'a
**son** k'ant
**song** yish
**sore throat** legash lazar
**sorry** bekhk ma billalah'
**sorry: I am sorry (to hear that).** Daala gesh doila.
**soul** sii
**sound equipment** zvukovoi ghirsa
**soup** chorpa
**sour** müst
**sour plum** müsta h'ach
**south** q'ilbi; yug
**souvenir shop** sowghata(n) tüka
**Soviet Union** Savyet Pachkhalq
**sow** den
**sowing** hush dh'a deer
**spade** bell
**spanner** mashena(n) doogha
**spare tire** zapaska
**speak** q'amel dan; **Do you speak English?** H'una Ingals mott biitsa kha'i?; **speak a language** motta biitsa
**speaker** dokladkho
**speaker of parliament** spiiker

**specialist** spetsiyalist
**speed** skorost
**spell: How do you spell that?** I(za) moagha yaaz do?
**spend** day'a
**spicy** k'oo
**spider** gezg
**spill** oah 'Caana(n); daarzha(n)
**spin** h'iizo
**spit** tuinash qiisa
**splint** (doctor's) shiina; (for broken limb) zöpar
**split** daat'a(n)
**spoil** talkha(n)
**sponge** gubka
**spoon** Caig (plural Caigash)
**sport** sport
**spread** daarzha(n)
**spring** bCästee
**spy** shpiyon
**stadium** stadiyon
**stale** kerla dootsu
**stallion** aighar
**stamp** marka; poshta(n) marka
**stand** hotta(n); latta(n); **to stand up** hotta(n); **Is the bridge still standing?** Tsun t'ökhal döödush t'ai hintsa lättash?
**star** seeda
**station: railway station** vogzal; **bus station** avtovogzal
**station** stantsi
**stationer's** kantselyarski tovarsh dukhka tüka
**stationer's** kantselyarski tüka
**statue** pamyatnik; statuya
**steal** q'oola dan
**steel** bolat
**steering wheel** rul
**sterling** funt sterling
**stethoscope** stetoskop
**stick** (verb) t'elato; **to stick to** lata(n)

**sting** yu tokha
**stingy** pis
**stink** h'ozha yan
**stitches** (*surgical*) chow dh'a teegar
**stomach** kiira
**stomachache** kiira lazar
**stone** t'ulg
**stop** satsa(n); **stop!** satsiita!
**stove** pesh
**straight** niisa; **straight on** niis(a) dh'a
**strange** tamashii
**stranger** khiira stag; khiira zuda
**strawberry** ts'azamash; **wild strawberry** toola
**stream** taatol
**street** uuram
**strength** nitsq'
**stretcher** nosilkash
**strike** (*noun*) zabastovka; bolkh oh'atasar; (*verb*) tookha(n); twokha(n)
**string** t'iirag
**strong** ch'oogha
**struggle** q'iisam; latar
**student** student
**subject** teema
**suburb** rayon
**success** ättoo
**such** ishtta
**sugar** sheekar
**suit** kostüm
**suitcase** chamda
**summer** äkhkee
**summit** boh'
**summon** qaiqa(n)
**sun** malkh
**Sunday** K'iran de
**sunglasses** küzganash
**sunny** malkh qetta; **It is sunny.** Malkha häzhna de(n) du.
**sunrise** sakhillar

**sunscreen** malkhekh lardesh dolu krem
**sunset** malkhbuzu khan
**supermarket** supermarket
**surgeon** khirurg
**surgery** operatsi
**surname** famili
**swamp** üshal
**swear** (*to take an oath*) dui baa; (*to curse*) sii dotsursh diitsa
**sweater** sviter
**sweep** nui h'akkha
**sweet** merza
**sweet pepper** q'oa yotsu burch
**sweetness** myerzalla
**swell** desta
**swim** neeka dan
**swimming** neeka
**swing** tekhka
**switch off** dh'a yai'a(n)
**switch on** s'h'allataya(n)
**synagogue** sinagoga
**syringe** maakha
**system** sistema

# T

**table** stol
**tablet** molkh; tabletka
**take** daaqqa(n); laatsa(n); **to take apart** vowshakh daaqqa(n)
**talk** (*noun*) khabar; (*verb*) q'amel dan
**tall** leqa(n)
**tampons** tamponash
**tank** bak; tank
**tap** kran
**tape** (*cassette*) kaseta
**tape recorder** magnitofon
**taste** h'azha
**tasteless** chaamaz

**tasty** merza; cham bolush

**Tat** Looman Zhütkii

**tax** nalog

**taxi** taksi

**tea** chai; **tea with lemon** limon tesna chai; **tea with milk** shura tökhna chai

**teach** h'eekha, ᶜaamoo

**teacher** h'ekharkho

**team** komanda

**tear** (*noun*) bᶜärkhi

**tear gas** bᶜärgekh khiish ökhiita gaz

**teaspoon** staka(n) ᶜaig

**teeth** tsergash

**telecommunications** telekommunikatsi

**telegram** telegrama

**telephone** telefon; **satellite phone** sputnika(n) telefon; **telephone center** telefon tsentr; (*verb*) telefon tookha(n)

**telescope** teleskop

**television** televideni; televizor; **television station** televidenin stantsi

**telex** teleks

**tell** aala(n)

**temperature** daagar

**temple** ghishlo

**ten** itt

**tent** palatka

**tent pegs** palatkiii(n) h'öqanash

**tenth** üttalgha

**termite** termit

**terrible** q'eemate

**thank** barkalla baakha(n)

**thank you** barkalla

**thanks** barkalla

**that** aalina; älla; bookhush; dᶜaaranig

**thaw** (*noun*) yashar

**the day after** qaana ciicha

**theater** teatar

**theft** q'oola; huma lachq'a yara

**their; theirs** shainig

**themselves** shäsh

**there** dᶜa; tsigah'; **is there?/are there?** yui/dui/bui?

**thermometer** termometar

**these** hworsh

**they** üsh; üzash

**thick** (*dense*) düq'a(n)

**thief** q'u

**thin** dutq'a(n)

**thing** huma

**think** oila ya(n)

**third** qo'algha; qwo'algha; **one third** qo'alagha daaq'a; **two thirds** qa'a deeq'akh shi'

**thirsty** h'agg; **I'm thirsty.** So h'agga wella/yella.

**thirteen** qoitta

**thirty** tq'ee itt

**this** hara

**those** dᶜaaranash

**thousand** ezar

**three** qo'; qwo'; **three times** quuza

**throat** legash

**thrombosis** tromb

**throw** qoossa(n); tasa(n)

**thumb** boqqa p'elg

**Thursday** Ye'arin (de)

**tick** (*insect*) vechchalg

**ticket** bilet

**ticket office** kassa

**tie** galstuk

**time** khan; **free time** müq'a khan; **What time is it?** Mas dälla wain?

**timetable** raspisani

**tire** ch'urg

**tired** k'add wala/yala

**tissues** salfetkash

**tobacco** t'onka

# twinkle

**today** takhan

**toe** kooga p'elg

**toilet** h'oshtagh; tualet; **toilet paper** tualeta(n) keekhat

**tomato** pomidor

**tomb** kash; **saint's tomb** ewlyaa'a(n) kash

**tomorrow** qaana; **the day after tomorrow** qaana ^ciicha; **tomorrow afternoon** qaan delq'khan t'iah'; **tomorrow morning** qaan ^cüiran; **tomorrow night** qaan sarah'

**tongue** mott

**tonight** tkhowsa

**too: too little** dukha kezzig/zhima; **too much/many** dukha dukha; duqqa duqa

**tool** instrument

**tooth** tserg

**toothache** tserg lazar

**toothbrush** tsergash yulu schötka

**toothpaste** tsergash yulu pasta

**toothpick** tsergakh ^cutturg

**top** böh'

**torture** staga(n) nitsqa ba; h'iiza war

**tourism** turizm

**tourist** turist; **tourist card** turista(n) kartochka

**tourniquet** turniket

**tow: Can you tow us?** Tkha mashen buksirtsa dh'a yugar yari ash?; **tow rope** buksiran mush; t'iirag

**towel** gata

**tower** t'eek'al dina tsa

**town center** ghalii(n) yuqq'e

**tower** ghaala; erza

**town** ghala

**tractor** traktor

**trade union** profsoyuz

**traditional** laamasta(n)

**traffic lights** svetofor

**train** poezd

**train station** poezda(n) vogzal

**training consultant** h'ekharna konsultant

**tranquilizer** trankvilizator

**transformer** transformator

**transfusion: blood transfusion** ts'ii dottar

**transmitter** peredachik

**trauma** chow, trauma

**travel** (*noun*) leelar; vaghar; (*verb*) leela(n); vagha(n)

**travel agent** bileta(n) kassa

**travelers' checks** dorozhni cheekash

**treacherous** meekara(n)

**tread** daala

**treasury** khazna

**tree** ditt

**trial** dow khattar

**tripwire** saargakh tesna yolu miina

**trolley bus** troleibus

**troops** salti

**trousers** khecha

**truce** masla^cat

**true** niisa

**truth** baq'derg

**try** h'azha

**Tuesday** Shinara

**turkey** moskal

**Turkish** Turkoin

**turn: turn left** ärroo aaghor verza/yerza; **turn right** ättoo aaghor vera/yerza

**twelve** shitta

**twentieth** tq'olgha; tq'algha

**twenty** tq'a

**twice** shozza

**twinkle** lyepa(n)

**twins** shal dina berash; shi yo<sup>c</sup>/ shi k'ant
**two** shi'
**type** taipa
**typewriter** pechatni mashen
**tyre** ch'urg

# U

**Ukrainian** Ukrainii(n)
**ulcer** da<sup>c</sup>; yazva
**umbrella** zontik
**uncomfortable** tsa parghat
**under** bukha; k'yela
**understand** qeeta; **I understand.** So qeeta.
**undertake** t'e laatsa
**underwear** chükhol yuugha humnash
**undo** s'h'a yasta
**unexploded bomb** eqqaz yolu bomba
**unhappy** reeza vootsush
**uniform** forma
**union: trade union** profsoyuz
**United Nations** O.O.N.
**university** universitet
**up** h'ala
**upriver** khin korta
**USA** Amerika

# V

**vaccinate: I have been vaccinated.** So vaktsinan maakha töghna wu/yu.
**valley** tooghee
**varnish** lak
**vase** vaaza
**vegetable shop** ovoshnoi tüka
**vegetables** khasstöömash

**vegetarian** vegetarianets
**vein** dega pkha
**veins** pkheenash
**venereal disease** venericheski tsamgar
**very** ch'oogha
**veto** veto
**vice-president** vitse-prezident
**video** videyo; (player) video-magnitofon
**video tape** video-kaseta
**view** surt
**village** yurt
**vinegar** uksus
**violence** t'om
**virus** virus
**visa** viza
**visitor** h'aasha
**vodka** q'arq'a
**voice** aaz
**voltage regulator** transformator
**vomit: I have been vomiting.** So cätta vina/yina.
**vote** (noun) qazh; (verb) kharzha
**vote-rigging** qazh tasar khartsa daqqar
**voting** qazh tasar

# W

**wage war** t'om ba(n)
**wait** h'azha(n)
**wake up** sam walla/yalla; **to wake someone up** sam waqqa/yaqqa
**wake-up call** sama waqqar
**Wales** Wels
**walkie-talkie** ratsiya
**wallet** bokhcha
**want: what do you want?** h'uuna hu yeeza?
**war** t'om; **to wage war** t'om ba(n)

**war crime(s)** t'ema zulm(ash)

**warm** yowkha

**war tribunal** t'ema sud

**war reparations** reparatsi

**wasp** z$^C$üüga

**watch** sah't

**watchmaker's** sah't toodesh mettig

**water** khi

**water bottle** khii(n) shisha

**waterfall** chukhchari

**watermelon** horbaz

**way** neq'; **this way** quzzagkhula; **that way** d$^C$agakhula

**we** (*exclusive*) tkho; (*inclusive*) vai

**weak** ghiila

**wear** duukha(n)

**weasel** shatq'a

**weather** pogoda; khena hottam

**Wednesday** Qa'ara

**week** k'ira; **last week** dh'a daghnacha k'irnah'; **next week** kera dooghacha k'irnah'; **this week** hoqa k'irnah'

**weekend** muq'dinosh

**weep** delkha

**welcome!** märsha wooghiil!

**well** (*of water*) mogush; ghu; (*adjective*) ghooläh'; (*adverb*) dika(n)

**Welsh** Welsii(n)

**west** malkhbuzi; zapad

**wet** (*adjective*) t'eda; (*verb*) t'ado

**what?** hun?; **what kind?** mülkha?; **what's that?** iza hu du?

**wheat** k'a

**wheel** ch'urg

**when?** matsa?

**where** michah'; styenga; **where is/are?** michah' wu/yu/du/bu?

**which?** mülkha?

**whisky** viski

**white** q'ai(n)

**who?** mila? (*plural* mülsh); **who to?** h'anna

**whole** derrig 'a

**why** hunda

**wide** shüüra

**widow** *see* **widowed**

**widowed:** *male* So wisna wu./ *female* So yisna yu.

**wife** zuda

**wild** aaqa(n)

**win** daqqa

**wind** (*noun*) mokh

**wind** (*verb*) t'e lista

**window** kor

**windscreen** h'alkhara küzg

**windy** mokh bälla

**wine** vino

**winter** $^C$a; $^C$an

**wire** saarg

**wisdom** h'eq'alalla

**wish** laa

**withdraw** aaradaqqa

**without** -za

**wolf** borz; bworz

**woman** zuda

**womb** beera(n) ts'a; gai

**wood** ditt; h'un; (*substance*) dechig

**wool** t'argha

**work** (*noun*) bolkh; bwolkh; ghullaq; (*verb*) bolkh ban

**world** $^C$aaläm; dünya

**worm** n$^C$ana

**worried** singattamii

**worry** sagatda(n)

**worse: I feel worse.** Suuna wookha kheeta.

**wound** choo yan

**wrench** mashena(n) doogha

**wrestling** oh' tooghar lattar

**wrist** ph'ars

**write** yaaz da(n)

**writer** yazdarkho
**writing paper** keekhat
**wrong: You are wrong.** H'o
   khartsa löö.

# Y

**yard** yard
**year** sho; shwo; **last year** stokhka;
**year: next year** ker dooghacha
   sharah'; **the year after next** shi
   sho dälcha; **the year before
   last** shi sho h'algha; **this year**
   hoqa sharah'
**yellow** moozha
**yes** ha'

**yesterday** selkha(n); syelkhana;
   **the day before yesterday**
   stoomar
**yoghurt** yetta(n) shura
**you** (*plural*) shu
**you** (*singular*) h'o; h'wo
**young** zhima
**your; yours** (*singular*) h'ainig;
   (*plural*) shainig
**yourself** (*singular*) h'wo
**yourselves** shäsh

# Z

**zero** nul
**zoo** zoopark

# CHECHEN
## PHRASEBOOK

## 1. ETIQUETTE

| | |
|---|---|
| Hello! | **As-salaamu ᶜalaikum!** |
| How are you? | **Moagha du ghullaqash?** |
| Fine, thank you. | **Dika du, barkalla.** |
| Good morning! | **ᶜÜrea dika yoila!** |
| Good afternoon! | **De dika doila!** |
| Good evening! | **Sürea dika yoila!** |
| Good night! | **Büsa dika yoila!** |
| See you tomorrow! | **Qaana gurdu wai!** |
| Goodbye! | **ᶜA dika yöila!** |
| Bon voyage! | **Neq dika khiila!** |
| Welcome  *to a male* | **Märsha wooghiil!** |
|            *to a female* | **Märsha yooghiil!** |
|            *to a group* | **Märsha dooghiil!** |

| | |
|---|---|
| yes | **ha'** |
| no | **haa-ha'** |
| thank you | **barkalla** |
| good luck! | **ättu boila!** |
| excuse me! | **bekhk ma billalah'!** |
| may I? | **megar dui?** |
| sorry! | **bekhk ma billalah'!** |

## 2. QUICK REFERENCE

| | |
|---|---|
| I | **so** |
| you *singular* | **h'o** |
| he/she/it | **i; iza** |
| we *exclusive* | **tkho** |
| we *inclusive* | **vai** |
| you *plural* | **shu** |
| they | **üsh; üzash** |
| | |
| this | **hara** |
| that | **d'aaranig** |
| these | **hworsh** |
| those | **d'aaranash** |
| | |
| here | **hoquzah'** |
| there | **d<sup>c</sup>a** |
| | |
| where? | **michah'?** |
| who? | **mila?** (*plural* **mülsh**) |
| what? | **hun?** |
| when? | **matsa?** |
| which? | **mülkha?** |
| how? | **moogha?** |
| why? | **hunda?** |
| how far? | **mel geena?** |
| how much? | **mel?** |
| how many? | **masa?** |
| what's that? | **iza hu du?** |
| is there?/are there? | **wui/yui/dui/bui?\*** |
| how near? | **mel ulläh'?** |
| where is/are? | **michah' wu/yu/du/bu?\*** |
| what must I do? | **as hu da deeza?** |
| what do you want? | **h'uuna hu yeeza?** |
| very | **ch'oogha** |

\* Depending on 'class' of thing referred – see page 8.

| | |
|---|---|
| and | **i; a** |
| or | **ya** |
| but | **amma** |

| | |
|---|---|
| I like/want . . . | **Suuna . . . veeza/yeeza/deeza/ beeza.*** |
| I don't like/want . . . | **Suuna . . . tsa veeza/yeeza/deeza/ beeza.*** |
| I know. | **Suuna kha'a.** |
| I don't know. | **Suuna tsa kha'a.** |
| Do you understand? | **H'o qeeti?** |
| I understand. | **So qeeta.** |
| I don't understand. | **So tsa qeeta.** |
| My condolences. | **Daala gesh doila.** |
| I am grateful. | **As barkalla booghu.** |
| It's important. | **Iza laarame ghullaq du.** |
| It doesn't matter. | **Humma dats.** |
| No problem! | **Q'aamil dats!** |
| more or less | **k'ezzig-duqa** |
| here is/are | **hara yu/wu/du/wu* h'uuna** |
| Is everything OK? | **Dika dui?** |
| Danger! | **Lar loo!** |
| How do you spell that? | **I(za) moogha yaaz do?** |

| | |
|---|---|
| I am. . . | **So . . .** |
| cold | **shell vella/yella.**** |
| hot | **vokh vella/yella.** |
| hungry | **mats vella/yella.** |
| thirsty | **h'agg vella/yella.** |
| happy | **reeza wu/yu.** |
| sad | **ghaighanii wu/yu.** |
| tired | **k'add vella/yella.** |
| well | **ghooläh' wu/yu.** |
| worried | **singattamii wu/yu.** |
| I am angry. | **So ööghaz vakhna.** |
| I am right. | **So baq' löö.** |
| I am sleepy. | **Suuna nab yookha.** |

\* See page 8.    \*\* **wu** = male speaker, **yu** = female speaker; see page 12.

## 2. INTRODUCTIONS

Chechens tend not to use titles such as Mr., Mrs., Ms., Miss, etc.

| | |
|---|---|
| What is your name? | **H'a ts'e hu yu?** |
| My name is . . . | **Sa ts'e . . . yu.** |
| (e.g. My name is Ahmad. | **Sa ts'e Ahmad yu.)** |
| May I introduce you to . . . | **Suuna h'o . . .-(a)na wowzita lä'ar.** |
| (e.g. May I introduce you to Ahmad. | **Suuna ho Ahmadana wowzita lä'ar.)** |
| This is my. . . | **Hara sa . . . wu/yu.** |
| friend | **dottagh** |
| colleague/companion | **naaq'ost** |
| (male) relative | **gergara stag** |
| (female) relative | **gergara zuda** |

## ABOUT YOURSELF. . .

### NATIONALITY

| | |
|---|---|
| Where are you from? | **H'o michh'ara wu/yu?** |
| I am from. . . | **So . . .-era wu/yu.** |
| | (e.g. **So Avstrali[era] wu.)** |
| Australia | **Avstrali** |
| Britain/England | **Angli** |
| Canada | **Kanada** |
| Ireland | **Irlandi** |
| New Zealand | **Novi Zilandi** |
| Northern Ireland | **Severni Irlandi** |
| Wales | **Wels** |
| Scotland | **Shotlandi** |
| the USA | **Amerika** |
| Europe | **Yevropa** |
| India | **Indi** |
| Japan | **Yaponi** |
| I am . . . | **So . . . wu/yu.** |
| American | **Amerikanets; Amerikii** |
| Australian | **Avstralii** |

| | |
|---|---|
| British/English | **Ingals, Anglii** |
| Canadian | **Kanadii** |
| Irish | **Irlandii** |
| Welsh | **Welsii** |
| Scottish | **Shotlandii** |

| | |
|---|---|
| Where were you born? | **H'o vina mettag hu yu?** |
| I was born in . . . | **So . . .-äh' vina wu/yu.** |

## CAUCASIAN NATIONALITIES

| | |
|---|---|
| Abkhaz | **Abkhaz** |
| Armenian | **Ermloi(n)** |
| Avar | **Sülii(n)** |
| Azeri | **Azerbaijani(n)** |
| Balkar | **Balkarii(n)** |
| Circassian | **Chergazii(n)** |
| Daghestani | **Sülii(n)** |
| Georgian | **Gürzhii(n)** |
| Ingush | **Ghalghai(n)** |
| Kabardian | **Gheebartoi(n)** |
| Kalmuk | **Ghalmaqii(n)** |
| Karachai | **Karachai(n)** |
| Kumyk | **Ghumqii(n)** |
| Lezgi | **Lezgi(n)** |
| Nogai | **Noghii(n)** |
| Tat/Mountain Jew | **Looman Zhütkii(n)** |

## OCCUPATIONS

| | |
|---|---|
| What do you do? | **H'o hu bolgh besh wu?** |
| I am a/an . . . | **So . . . wu/yu.** |
|     academic | **ᶜilmancha** |
|     accountant | **bukhgalter** |
|     administrator | **küigalkho** |
|     agronomist | **agronom** |
|     aid worker | **gumanitarni gho desh wola belghalo** |

| | |
|---|---|
| architect | **arkhitektor** |
| artist | **isbäh'alcha** |
| business person | **biznismen** |
| carpenter | **dechig-ph'ar** |
| consultant | **konsultant** |
| dentist | **tsergii(n) lor** |
| diplomat | **diplomat** |
| doctor | **lor** |
| economist | **ekonomist** |
| engineer | **inginer** |
| farmer | **fermer** |
| film-maker | **kinorezhisser** |
| journalist | **zhurnalist** |
| lawyer | **advokat** |
| manual worker | **küiga belghalo** |
| mechanic | **mekhanik** |
| negotiator | **yuq'alelarg; mediyator** |
| nurse | **medsestra** |
| observer | **tidamcho** |
| officer worker | **ofis-belghalo** |
| pilot | **lyotchik** |
| political scientist | **politolog** |
| scientist | **ᶜilmancha** |
| secretary | **secretar** |
| soldier | **salti** |
| student | **student** |
| surgeon | **khirurg** |
| teacher | **h'ekharkho** |
| telecommunications specialist | **telekommunikatsii(n) spetsiyalist** |
| tourist | **turist** |
| training consultant | **h'ekharna konsultant** |
| writer | **yazdarkho** |

## INTRODUCTIONS

### AGE

| | |
|---|---|
| How old are you? | **H'a mass sho du?** |
| I am . . . years old. | **Sa . . . sho du.** |

### FAMILY

| | | |
|---|---|---|
| Are you married? | m | **Ho zuda yaliina wui?** |
| | f | **Ho marriah' yui ?** |
| I am single. | m | **So zuda yaloz wu.** |
| | f | **So marre yaghaz yu.** |
| I am married. | m | **So zuda yalina wu.** |
| | f | **So marriah' yu.** |
| I am divorced. | m | **Zuda yitana wu so.** |
| | f | **So yitana yu.** |
| I am widowed. | m | **So wisna wu.** |
| | f | **So yisna yu.** |
| Do you have a boyfriend? | | **Ha t'e h'iiza k'ant wui?** |
| Do you have a girlfriend? | | **Ha t'e h'iiza yoᶜ yui?** |
| What is his/her name? | | **Tsün ts'e hu yu?** |
| How many children do you have? | | **H'a mas beera du?** |
| I don't have any children. | | **Sa beerash da' dats.** |
| I have a daughter. | | **Sa yoᶜ yu** |
| I have a son. | | **Sa k'ant wu.** |
| How many sisters do you have? | | **Ha mas washa wu?** |
| How many brothers do you have? | | **Ha mas yisha yu?** |

| | | |
|---|---|---|
| father | | **da(n)** |
| mother | | **nana** |
| grandfather | *father's side* | **de(n) da(n)** |
| | *mother's side* | **nena da(n)** |
| grandmother | *father's side* | **de(n) nana** |
| | *mother's side* | **nena nana** |
| brother | | **washa** |
| sister | | **yisha** |

| | |
|---|---|
| children | **beerash** |
| daughter | **yo<sup>c</sup>** |
| son | **k'ant** |
| twins | **shal dina beerash;** |
| | *girls* **shi yo<sup>c</sup>**; *boys* **shi k'ant** |
| husband | **mar** |
| wife | **zuda** |
| family | **dözal** |
| man | **stag** |
| woman | **zuda** |
| boy | **k'ant** |
| girl | **zhima yo<sup>c</sup>** |
| person | **stag; adam** |
| people | **nakh** |

## RELIGION

The Chechens are a Sunni Muslim people. Integral not only to their religious way of life but also secular, political and so on, are the Sufi sects or 'paths' – the Naqshbandi and the Qadiri – to which many adults owe allegiance (for more, see the note on 'Religious Heritage' on page 127).

| | |
|---|---|
| What is your religion? | **H'o mülghcha dinah' wu/yu?** |
| I am (a) . . . | **So . . . wu/yu.** |
|    Muslim | **Busurban** |
|    Buddhist | **Buddist** |
|    Orthodox | **Kerstan** |
|    Christian | **Kerstan** |
|    Hindu | **Indusii(n)** |
|    Jewish | **Zhügtii(n)** |

| | |
|---|---|
| Islam | **Islam; Busurba Dina** |
| Buddhism | **Buddizm** |
| Christianity | **Kerstan dina** |
| Hinduism | **Indusii(n) dina** |
| Judaism | **Zhügtii(n) dina** |
| I am not religious. | **So deelah' teshash wats/yats.*** |

* Literally: 'I do not believe in God.'

## 4. LANGUAGE/MOTT

Aside from the other indigenous languages spoken in the Caucasus, everyone speaks Russian. Many will also know a smattering at least of one or more European languages — such as German and English, while the older generations tend to know French. Because of the Chechen diaspora as well as the obvious influence of Islam, you will find quite a few speakers of Arabic and Turkish.

| | |
|---|---|
| Do you speak English? | **H'una Ingals mott biitsa kha'i?** |
| Do you speak Russian? | **H'una Örsiin mott biitsa kha'i?** |
| Do you speak German? | **H'una Nemtsoin mott biitsa kha'i?** |
| Do you speak French? | **H'una Frantsuziin mott biitsa kha'i?** |
| Do you speak Arabic? | **H'una ᶜArbiin mott biitsa kha'i?** |
| Do you speak Turkish? | **H'una Turkoin mott biitsa kha'i?** |

| | |
|---|---|
| Does anyone speak English? | **Ts'h'annena Ingals mott biitsa kha'i?** |
| I speak a little . . . | **Suna ts'h'a zhimma . . . mott biitsa kha'a.** |
| I don't speak. . . | **Suna . . . mott biitsa tsa kha'a.** |
| I understand. | **So qeeta.** |
| I don't understand. | **So tsa qeeta.** |

| | |
|---|---|
| Please point to the word in the book. | **I dosh kinshkit'yah' michah' du gaitah'.** |
| Please wait while I look up the word. | **Otsu deshna mä'na hu du h'azhaltsa soobar de.** |
| Could you speak more slowly, please? | **Mellash diitsa megar dari ah'?** |
| Could you repeat that? | **Iz yugha alah'?** |
| How do you say . . . in Chechen? | **. . . moogha era dar?** |
| What does . . . mean? | **. . . bogharg hu du?** |
| How do you pronounce this word? | **I dosh moogha oola 'ah'?** |

| I speak . . . | As . . . mott büitsa. |
|---|---|
| Arabic | ᶜArbiin |
| Armenian | Ermaloin |
| Azeri | Azerbeijaniin |
| Danish | Datkhoin |
| Dutch | Gollandkhoin |
| English | Ingals(an) |
| French | Frantsuziin |
| Georgian | Gürzhiin |
| German | Nemtsoin |
| Greek | Grekiin |
| Italian | Italianiin |
| Japanese | Yaponiin |
| Ossete | Hiriin |
| Ukrainian | Ukrainiin |
| Russian | Örsiin; (*less polite:* Ghaazaqiin) |
| Turkish | Turkoin |

## 5. BUREAUCRACY

Note that the details below are purely for reference purposes, since any form you encounter will be written in Russian.

### FILLING IN FORMS

| | |
|---|---|
| name | **ts'e** |
| address | **adres** |
| date of birth | **vina de(n)** |
| place of birth | **vina mettig** |
| nationality | **grazhdanalla** |
| age | **khan** |
| sex: male | **börsha** |
| female | **ste** |
| religion | **din** |
| reason for travel: | **waara bah'na** |
| business | **ghullaq; biznis** |
| tourism | **turizm** |
| work | **bolkh; ghullaq** |
| personal | **she(n) doolah' dolu** |
| profession | **kormatalla, professi** |
| marital status | **dözal khilar** |
| single | *m* **zuda yaaliaz** |
| | *f* **maari yaghaz** |
| married | *m* **zuda yaalin** |
| | *f* **maariah'** |
| divorced | *m* **wisna** |
| | *f* **yitana** |
| date | **de** |
| date of arrival | **s'h'a qoocha de** |
| date of departure | **dh'a wööda de** |
| passport | **pasport** |
| passport number | **pasportan nomer** |
| visa | **viza** |
| currency | **valyuta** |

## MINISTRIES

Ministries and most other departments and official organisations are referred to by their names or acronyms in Russian – a natural occurrence, since Russian is the language of bureaucracy.

| | |
|---|---|
| Ministry of Defense | **Ministerstvo Oboroni** |
| Ministry of Agriculture | **Minselkhoz** |
| Ministry of Home Affairs | **MVD ('em-ve-de')** |
| Ministry of Foreign Affairs | **MID ('miid')** |
| Ministry of Transport | **Minesterstvo transporta** |
| Ministry of Health | **Minzdrav** |
| Ministry of Education | **Ministerstvo Obrazovanya** |
| Ministry of Justice | **Ministerstvo Yustitsii** |

## USEFUL PHRASES

| | |
|---|---|
| Is this the correct form? | **Hara keekhat niisa dui?** |
| What does this mean? | **I booghurg hu du?** |
| Where is . . .'s office? | **. . .-ii(n) kabinet michah' yu?** |
| Which floor is it on? | **Mülghacha etazh t'iyah' yu iz?** |
| Does the lift work? | **Lift bolkh besh yui?** |
| Is Mr./Ms. . . . in? | **. . . choh' wui/yui?** |
| Please tell him/her that I am here. | **So quzah' wu/yu aalah' tsünga.** |
| I can't wait, I have an appointment. | **Sa quzah' ⁽ᶜ⁾ea yish yats. Sa wagha veezash mettigash yu.** |
| Tell him/her that I was here. | **So ve'nera aalalah' tsünga.** |

## 6. TRAVEL

**Public transport** — When running, buses are generally too crammed as to be impractical. Far more practical are taxis or private cars hailed in the street. Travel by rail is slow, subject to long delays mid-journey and less safe than by road. Note that all public announcements, particularly for trains and planes, are made in Russian. Bicycles are difficult to find.

### ENQUIRIES

| | |
|---|---|
| What time does (the) . . . leave/arrive? | **. . . mas dälcha dh'a döda/s'h'a qoocha?** |
| the airplane | **kema dh'a dööda?** |
| the boat | **kema(korabal) dh'a dööda?** |
| the bus | **avtobus dh'a yööda?** |
| the train | **poezd dh'a bööda?** |
| the trolley bus | **troleibus yööda?** |
| The plane is delayed/ cancelled. | **Kema t'äh' büsa/tsa bööda.** |
| The train is delayed/ cancelled. | **Poezd t'äh' düsa/tsa dööda.** |
| How long will it be delayed? | **Iza mellana t'äh' büsash bu?** |
| There is a delay of . . . hours. | **. . . sah'tan t'äh' bisar khila.** |

### BUYING TICKETS

| | |
|---|---|
| Excuse me, where is the ticket office? | **Bekhk ma billalah', kassa michah' yu?** |
| Where can I buy a ticket? | **Bilet michah' öötsar dar as?** |
| I want to go to. . . | **So . . . vagha veza.** |
| I want a ticket to . . . | **Suuna . . . q'achchalts'a bilet deeza.** |
| I would like . . . | **Suuna . . . deeza** |
| a one-way ticket | **dh'a vagha bilet** |
| a return ticket | **dh'ai-s'h'ai vagha bilet** |
| first class | **SV ('es-ve' – *trains*)** |

| | |
|---|---|
| second class | **platskartni** |
| business class | **kupeini** |

| | |
|---|---|
| Do I pay in dollars or roubles? | **Dollarsh loo as ya söömash?** |
| You must pay in dollars. | **Dollarsh dal deeza ah'.** |
| You must pay in roubles. | **Söömash dal deeza ah'.** |
| You can pay in either. | **Mülkha delcha be'a dats.** |
| Can I reserve a place? | **Ts'h'an mettagan bronn ya megar dui?** |
| How long does the trip take? | **Nowq'ah' mel khan yaqqa yeeza?** |
| Is it a direct route? | **Khiitsam bootsush märshrut yui 'i?** |

## AIR

In Russia all flights are (technically) non-smoking.

| | |
|---|---|
| Is there a flight to . . .? | **. . . yöödash reis yui?** |
| When is the next flight to . . .? | **. . . yöödash sholgha reis mas dälcha yu?** |
| How long is the flight? | **Kema dh'a mass sah'täh' dööda?** |
| What is the flight number? | **Reisan nomer hu yu?** |
| You must check in at . . . | **. . . sah't dälcha registratsi ya yeza 'ah'.** |

| | |
|---|---|
| Is the flight delayed? | **Kema t'iah' düsush dui?** |
| How many hours is the flight delayed? | **Mas sah'tan t'iah' düsushdu kema?** |
| Is this the flight for . . . ? | **Hara kema . . . dödush dui?** |
| Is that the flight from . . . ? | **Hara kema . . .-eera dooghush dui?** |
| When is the Moscow flight arriving? | **Moskvar kema mas dälcha s'h'a qoocha?** |
| Is it on time? | **Kheenah' dooghush dui iz?** |

| | |
|---|---|
| Is it late? | **T'iah' düsush dui iz?** |
| Do I have to change planes? | **Kema kheetsa deezi sai?** |
| Has the plane left Moscow yet? | **Moskvar kema h'al ghättani?** |
| What time does the plane take off? | **Mas dälcha h'al ghotta kema?** |
| What time do we arrive in Moscow? | **Moskva wai mas dälcha dh'a qoocha?** |

| | |
|---|---|
| excess baggage | **sow bagazh** |
| international flight | **qeecha pachkhalqe döödu kema** |
| internal flight | **chöh'aara kema/reis** |

## BUS

| | |
|---|---|
| bus stop | **avtobusan ostanovka** |
| Where is the bus stop/station? | **Avtobusan ostanovka/ avtovogzal michah' yu?** |
| Take me to the bus station. | **So avtovogzale wigah'/yigah'.** |
| Which bus goes to ...? | **Mülgha avtobus ... yööda?** |
| Does this bus go to ...? | **Har avtobus ... yöödi?** |
| How often do buses pass by? | **Avtobus massoz yööda quzagkhoola?** |
| What time is the ... bus? | **... avtobus mas dälcha yöödu?** |
| next | **sholgha** |
| first | **döhh'ar** |
| last | **tähh'ar** |
| Will you let me know when we get to ...? | **Wai ...-e qächcha kha'itar dari 'ah' sööga?** |
| Stop, I want to get off! | **Sats yeelah'! So quzah' oh' wossa veza/yeza!** |
| Where can I get a bus to ...? | **... t'e yööda avtobus michah' karoora yar suuna?** |
| When is the first bus to ...? | **... yööda döhh'ar avtobus mas dälcha yu?** |

| | |
|---|---|
| When is the last bus to . . . ? | **. . . yööda tähh'ar avtobus mas dälcha yu?** |
| When is the next bus to . . . ? | **. . . yööda sholgha avtobus matsa yu?** |
| Do I have to change buses? | **Avtobus kheetsa yeeza sa?** |
| I want to get off at . . . | **So . . . t'iah' oh'a woss veeza /yeeza.** |
| Please let me off at the next stop. | **Sholgha ostanovkyah' so 'oh'a wossitalah'.** |
| Please let me off here. | **So quzah' oh'a wossitah'.** |
| How long is the journey? | **Mas sah'teh' neq ba beeza wai?** |
| What is the fare? | **Hu döögha biletah'?** |
| I need my luggage, please. | **Sai humnash s'h'a eetsa megar dui?** |
| That's my bag. | **Iza sa törmag bu.** |

## TRAIN

| | |
|---|---|
| Passengers must. . . | **Pasazhirash . . .** |
| change trains. | **poezd kheetsa beeza.** |
| change platforms. | **platforma kheetsa yeeza.** |
| Is this the right platform for . . . ? | **Hara . . . bööda poezdan platform yui?** |
| The train leaves from platform . . . | **Poezd . . . platformeera dh'a böödash bu.** |
| Is there a timetable? | **Raspisani yui quzah'?** |
| Take me to the railway station. | **So vogzale wigah'/yigah'.** |
| Which platform should I go to? | **So mülkhacha platforme wagha veeza?** |
| platform one/two | **döhh'ar/sholgha platforme** |
| You must change trains at . . . | **. . . gah' poezd kheetsa beeza ah'.** |
| Where can I buy tickets? | **Bilet michah' öötsur dar as?** |

| Will the train leave on time? | **Poezd kheenah' dh'a ghuura bui?** |
| There will be a delay of minutes. | **. . . minotan t'iah' büsu poezd.** |
| There will be a delay of . . . hours. | **. . . sah'tan t'iah' büsu poezd.** |

## TAXI

Some taxis are marked , while others are not. You can also wave down and negotiate a fare with any private car willing to go your way, although this is not always as safe. To avoid unpleasant surprises, agree to fares in advance, with tip included. It is useful to be able to tell the driver your destination in Chechen or Russian (or have it written down on a piece of paper), as many speak nothing else. Be warned, however, that some drivers will have as little idea as you as to the precise whereabouts of your destination.

| Taxi! | **Taksi!** |
| Where can I get a taxi? | **Taksi michah' karor yar suuna?** |
| Please could you get me a taxi. | **Suuna taksi laatsah'.** |
| Can you take me to. . .? | **So . . . vügar vari 'ah'?** |
| Please take me to . . . | **So . . . vigh'aara 'ah'?** |
| How much will it cost it to. . .? | **. . . qachchaltsa vagha hu dala deeza?** |
| To this address, please. | **Hoqa adrese vigah' so.** |
| Turn left. | **Ärroo aaghor verza.** |
| Turn right. | **Ättoo aaghor verza.** |
| Go straight ahead. | **Niisa dh'a.** |
| Stop! | **Satsiita!** |
| Don't stop! | **Ma satslah'!** |
| I'm in a hurry. | **So sikha wu/yu.** |
| Please drive more slowly! | **Ts'h'a zhimma mellish yaghiitah' (mashen)!** |
| Here is fine, thank you. | **Quzah' sats yeelah'.** |

| The next corner, please. | **Sholghacha mäᶜnäh' sats yeelah'.** |
| The next street to the left. | **Ättuu aaghorah' bolu sholgha uuram.** |
| The next street to the right. | **Ärruu aaghorah' bolu sholgha uuram.** |
| Stop here! | **Quzh' sats yeelah'!** |
| Stop the car, I want to get out. | **Quzh' sats yeelah' mashen, so oh' wossa veeza/yeeza.** |
| Please wait here. | **Quzah' soobar deelah'.** |
| Take me to the airport. *m* | **So aeroporte wigah'.** |
| *f* | **So aeroporte yigah'.** |

## GENERAL PHRASES

| I want to get off at . . . | **So . . .-ah' oh' wossa veeza/yeeza.** |
| Excuse me! | **Bekhk ma billalah'!** |
| Excuse me, may I get by? | **Bekhk ma billalah', cheq vaala/yaala megar dui?** |
| These are my bags. | **Horsh sa törmagash bu./ Hara sa bagazh yu.** |
| Please put them there. | **Hoqquz oh'a dekhkah' üsh.** |
| Is this seat free? | **Hara mettag dh'a lätsna yui?** |
| I think that's my seat. | **Hara sa mettig yu.** |

## EXTRA WORDS

| ambulance | **skori pomosh** |
| bicycle | **vilispet** |
| boat | **kema** |
| car | **mashen** |
| 4-wheel drive | **shi' privod yölu mashen** |
| helicopter | **vertolyot** |
| horse and cart | **gowr i wordi** |
| motorbike | **mototsikal** |
| trolley bus | **troleibus** |
| airport | **aeroport** |
| airport tax | **aeroportan nalog** |
| arrivals | **s'h'aqaachar** |

| | |
|---|---|
| baggage counter | **bagazhni sektsi** |
| boarding pass | **posadkin talon** |
| bus stop | **avtobusan ostanovka** |
| cancellation | **dh'a daqqar** |
| check-in counter | **registratsiin sektsi** |
| check-in | **registratsi** |
| closed | **q'oilana;** *Russian* **zakrito** |
| customs | **tamozhni** |
| delay | **t'iah' disar** |
| departures | **dh'adaghar** |
| dining car | **vagon-restoran** |
| emergency exit | **avariini aaradovliila\*** |
| entrance | **chughoila \*** |
| exit | **aaradovliila\*** |
| express | **skoryi** |
| ferry | **buram** |
| information | **spravochni** |
| ladies/gents | **zudariin/bozhariin** |
| local (for trains) | **elektrichka** |
| no entry | *Russian* **nyet vkhoda** |
| no smoking | *Russian* **ne kurit** |
| open | **yillana;** *Russian* **otkrito** |
| path | **taacha** |
| platform number | **platformi(n) nomer** |
| railway | **ächka neq'** |
| reserved | *Russian* **zanyato** |
| road | **neq'** |
| sign | **znak; kha'am** |
| sleeping car | **kupe yolu vagon** |
| station | **stantsi** |
| telephone | **telefon** |
| ticket office | **kassa** |
| timetable | **raspisani** |
| toilets | **tualet; hoshtagh** |
| town center | **ghaliin yuqq'e** |
| train station | **poezdan vogzal** |

\* The Russian forms are usually used.

# 7. ACCOMMODATION

Should accommodation be found, you will find that room service is not available, and breakfast or other meals will have to be negotiated and paid for separately.

| | |
|---|---|
| I am looking for a . . . | **So . . . lööghush wu/yu.** |
| guesthouse | **gostinitsa; h'eesha ts'a** |
| hotel | **gostinitsa** |
| hostel | **turbaza** |
| Is there anywhere I can stay for the night? | **Büsa yaqqa mettig yui quzah'?** |
| Is there anywhere we can stay for the night? | **Tkhuna tkhowsa büüsa yaqqa mettig yui quzah'?** |
| Where is. . . | **. . . michah' yu?** |
| a cheap hotel | **yoorakh gostinitsa** |
| a good hotel | **dika(n) gostinitsa** |
| a nearby hotel | **ulläh' yolu gostinitsa** |
| a clean hotel | **ts'ena gostinitsa** |
| What is the address? | **Hu du tsüna adres?** |
| Could you write the address please? | **Tsüna adres yaazdira dari 'ah'?** |

## AT THE HOTEL

| | |
|---|---|
| Do you have any rooms free? | **Shu ts'h'aa yeesa chöö yui?** |
| I would like. . . | **Suuna . . . yeeza.** |
| a single room | **ts'h'a' vüzhush chöö** |
| a double room | **shi' vuzhush chöö** |
| We'd like a room. | **Ts'h'a chöö yezar tkhuna.** |
| We'd like two rooms. | **Shi chöö yezar tkhuna.** |
| I want a room with . . . | **Suuna . . . yolush chöö yeeza.** |
| a bathroom | **vanni** |
| a shower | **dush** |
| a television | **televizor** |
| a window | **kor** |

# ACCOMMODATION

| | |
|---|---|
| a double bed | **boqqa mänga** |
| a balcony | **balkon** |
| I want a room that's quiet. | **Choh' ghowgha tsa khezash yolu chöö yeezar suuna.** |
| How long will you be staying? | **H'o mell ᶜee dagah' wu/yu?** |
| How many nights? | **Mass büüsa?** |
| I'm going to stay for. . . | **So . . . sotsar wu/yu.** |
| one day | **ts'h'an diinah'** |
| two days | **shin diinah'** |
| one week | **ts'h'an k'irnah'** |
| Do you have any I.D.? | **H'öögiah' ts'h'aa dokument dui?** |
| Sorry, we're full. | **Bekhk ma billalah', tkha qi mettag yats** |
| I have a reservation. | **Sa bronn yu.** |
| My name is . . . | **Sa ts'e . . . yu.** |
| May I speak to the manager please? | **Administratoreg/Direktoreg q'amel da megar dui as?** |
| I have to meet someone here. | **Ts'h'a' ga vezash wu/yu so.** |
| How much is it per night/ per person? | **Hu döögha horranegha ts'h'a büüsa yoqqarga?** |
| How much is it per week? | **K'irnakh hu döögha?** |
| It's . . . per day/per person. | **. . . hoora diinah'/büsa** |
| Can I see it? | **H'azha megar dui tsünga?** |
| Are there any others? | **Qi yui shügah'?** |
| Is there . . . ? | **Quzah' . . .** |
| air conditioning | **konditsiyoner yui?** |
| laundry service | **humnash yüttu mettig yui?** |
| room service | **nomeran servis yui?** |
| a telephone | **telefon yui?** |
| hot water | **dowgha khi dui?** |
| No, I don't like it. _m_ | **So reeza wats tsuna.** |
| _f_ | **So reeza yats tsuna.** |

| It's too . . . | Iza duqa . . . yu. |
|---|---|
| cold | shiila |
| hot | yowkha |
| big | yoqqa |
| dark | ⁿärzha |
| small | zhima |
| noisy | ghowghana |
| dirty | böögha |

| | |
|---|---|
| It's fine, I'll take it. | Dika du, as s'h'a 'öötsa iza. |
| Where is the bathroom? | Vanni michah' yu? |
| Is there hot water all day? | Dowgha khi diinah' sarraltsa dooghi? |
| Do you have a safe? | Seif yui shu? |
| Is there anywhere to wash clothes? | Humnash yitta mettag yui shu? |
| Can I use the telephone? | Telefon toogha megar dui? |

## NEEDS

| I need . . . | Suuna . . . öösha. |
|---|---|
| candles | ch'uuram |
| toilet paper | tualetan keekhat |
| soap | saba |
| clean sheets | ts'ena shärshonash |
| an extra blanket | qi ts'h'a yurkha |
| drinking water | molu khi |
| a light bulb | stogar |

| | |
|---|---|
| Please wake me up at . . . (o'clock). | So . . . (sah't dälcha) h'al ghattur wari 'ah'. |
| Please change the sheets. | Motta kheetsah'. |
| I can't open/close the window. | Kor s'h'a tsa dellalo/dh'a tsa q'owlalo sööga. |
| I have lost my key. | As sai doogha dai'ana. |
| Can I have the key to my room? | San chööna doogha h'a looh'a? |

# ACCOMMODATION

| | |
|---|---|
| The toilet won't flush. | **Tualet chura khi oh' tsa dööda.** |
| I am leaving now. | **So dh'a vöödush vu.** |
| We are leaving now. | **Tkho dh'a dölghush du.** |
| | |
| I would like to pay the bill. | **Makh dh'a balla lä'är suuna.** |
| wake-up call | **sama waqqar** |
| I would like to be woken up at . . . (o'clock). | **So . . . (sah't dälcha) sama waqqa veeza/yeeza.** |
| The water has been cut off. | **Khi setsna.** |
| The electricity has been cut off. | **Svyet dh'a yalla/dh'a khaadiina.** |
| The gas has been cut off. | **Gaz dh'a khaadiina.** |
| The heating has been cut off. | **Otopleni dh'a khaadiina/dh'a yalla.** |
| The heater doesn't work. | **Pesh bolkh besh yats.** |
| The air conditioning doesn't work. | **Konditsiyoner bolkh besh yats.** |
| The phone doesn't work. | **Telefon bolkh besh yats.** |
| I can't flush the toilet. | **Tualet choh' khi oh'a tsa dööda.** |
| The toilet is blocked. | **Tualet dh'a yuq'na.** |
| I can't switch off the tap. | **Kran dh'a tsa q'owla lo.** |

## EXTRA WORDS

| | |
|---|---|
| bathroom | **vanni** |
| bed | **mänga** |
| bill | **makh; schyot** |
| blanket | **yurkha** |
| candle | **ch'uuram** |
| chair | **ghant** |
| clean | **ts'ena** |
| cold water | **shiila khi** |
| cupboard | **ishkap** |
| dark | **ᶜärzha** |
| dirty | **böögha** |

| | |
|---|---|
| doorlock | **doogha** |
| double bed | **boqqa mänga** |
| electricity | **svet; elektrichestvo** |
| excluded | **dootsush/yootsush** |
| fridge | **kholodilnik** |
| hot/cold | **dowgha/shiila** |
| hot water | **dowgha khi** |
| included | **dolush/yolush** |
| key | **doogha** |
| laundry | **prachechni** |
| mattress | **göö** |
| meals | **ya'a huma** |
| mirror | **küzga** |
| name | **ts'e** |
| noisy | **ghowgha yölu** |
| padlock | **doogha** |
| pillow | **ghaiba** |
| plug | **rozetka** |
| quiet | **tiina** |
| room | **chöö; nomer** |
| room number | **chöö(n) nomer** |
| shampoo | **shampun** |
| sheet | **shärshuu** |
| shower | **dush** |
| suitcase | **chamda** |
| surname | **famili** |
| table | **stol** |
| towel | **gata** |
| water | **khi** |
| window | **kor** |

**Electric current** — Chechnya is **220**-volt electric current. However, it may not be constantly at full voltage strength and lengthy power failures may be common, particularly away from Grozny, where each village has its own local transformer, which can overload. Although many buildings may now have their own back-up generators in case of power failure, be sure to keep a flashlight or supply of candles.

## 8. FOOD AND DRINK

Food plays an important part of Chechen life, and important events in all aspects of life and the year are marked with a feast of one form or another. In normal times, you will be offered a dazzling variety of dishes, delicacies and drinks, which vary from area to area and from season to season. Any menu you may encounter will be written in Russian.

### MEALS

| | |
|---|---|
| breakfast | **marta; zavtrak** |
| lunch | **delq'an yu'urg; obed** |
| snack | **zakuska** |
| dinner, supper | **ph'or** |
| dessert | **desert** |

| | |
|---|---|
| I'm hungry. | **So metsa wu/yu.** |
| *or* | **So mats vella/yella.** |
| I'm thirsty. | **So h'agga wella/yella.** |

| | |
|---|---|
| Ramadan | **Markhiin Butta** |
| I am fasting. | **Sa markha du.** |
| to break a fast | **markha dasta** |

### EATING OUT

| | |
|---|---|
| Do you know a good restaurant? | **Dika restoran yolu mettag kha'i h'uuna?** |
| I would like a table for . . . please. | **. . . stagan stol yeezar suuna.** |

| | |
|---|---|
| Can I see the menu please? | **Menüga h'azha megar dui?** |
| I'm still looking at the menu. | **So menü t'iah' hu yu h'ozhush wu/yu.** |
| I would like to order now. | **Suuna zakaz ya lä'a.** |
| What's this? | **Iza hu yu?** |
| Is it spicy? | **K'oa yui iza?** |
| Does it have meat in it? | **Zhizhigakh humma yui tsu yuqq'äh'?** |

| | |
|---|---|
| Does it have alcohol in it? | **Alkogol tökha yui 'iza?** |
| Do you have . . . ? | **Shügah' . . . yui?** |
| We don't have . . . | **Tkhoigah' . . . yats/dats/bats.*** |
| What would you recommend? | **H'uuna khetareh' hu yegha megar dar?** |
| Do you want . . . ? | **H'uuna . . . yeezi/deezi/beezi*?** |
| Can I order some more . . . ? | **. . . qi'a yegha megar dui?** |
| That's all, thank you. | **Tö'ar du, barkalla h'uuna.** |
| | |
| That's enough, thanks. | **Qi tsa ööshu, barkalla.** |
| I haven't finished yet. | **So hintsa yi'na tsa wälla/ yälla.** |
| I have finished eating. | **So yi'na wälla/yälla.** |
| I am full up! | **So vüzna/yüzna.** |
| Where are the toilets? | **Tualet michah' yu?** |
| | |
| I am a vegetarian. | **So vegetarianets wu/yu.** |
| I don't eat meat. | **As zhizhig tsa du'u.** |
| I don't eat pork. | **So h'äqi zhizhig du'ush wats/ yats.** |
| I don't eat chicken or fish. | **As kootam ya ch'aara tsa bu'u.** |
| I don't drink alcohol. | **So molush wats/yats.** |
| I don't smoke. | **So uuzush wats/yats.** |
| | |
| I would like . . . | **Suuna . . . yeeza.** |
| an ashtray | **chimtosurg (yeeza)** |
| the bill | **shchöt (yeeza)** |
| a glass of water | **khin stakan (deeza)** |
| a bottle of water | **khin shisha (deeza)** |
| a bottle of wine | **vinon shisha (deeza)** |
| a bottle of beer | **pivan shisha (deeza)** |
| another bottle | **qi ts'h'a shisha (deeza)** |
| a bottle-opener | **otkrivalka (yeeza); t'us s'h'a bosturg (beeza)** |

* Depending on 'class' of thing referred – see page 8.

## EXTRA WORDS

| | |
|---|---|
| a corkscrew | **shtopor** |
| a cup | **kad; chashka** |
| dessert | **desert** |
| a drink | **mala huma** |
| a fork | **ma<sup>c</sup>ar** |
| another chair | **qi ts'h'a ghant** |
| another plate | **qi ts'h'a kheedar** |
| another glass | **qi ts'h'a staka(n)** |
| another cup | **qi ts'h'a chashka** |
| a napkin | **kekhatan salfetka/gata** |
| a glass | **staka** |
| a knife | **urs** |
| a plate | **kheedar** |
| samovar | **samovar** |
| a spoon | **<sup>c</sup>aig** |
| table | **stol** |
| teaspoon | **stakan <sup>c</sup>aig** |
| toothpick | **tsergakh <sup>c</sup>utturg** |

| | |
|---|---|
| fresh | **kerla** |
| spicy | **k'oo** |
| stale | **kerla dootsu** |
| sour | **müst** |
| sweet | **merza** |
| hot | **yowkha** |
| cold | **shiila** |
| salty | **düra** |
| tasteless | **chaamaz** |
| bad | **gho** |
| tasty | **merza; cham bolush** |

| | |
|---|---|
| too much | **dukha dukha** |
| too little | **dukha kezzig/zhima** |
| not enough | **tsa tö'ush** |

## FOOD

| | |
|---|---|
| bread | **beepig** |
| caviar | **ikra** |
| cheese | **nekhcha** |
| chewing gum | **seeghaz** |
| egg | **kho'** |
| flour | **dama** |
| french fries | **qärzna kartolgash** |
| honey | **mwaz** |
| ice cream | **morozhni** |
| ketchup | **kechup** |
| mustard | **gorchitsa** |
| nut | **b'aar** |
| oil | **dätta** |
| pasta | **garznash** |
| pepper | **burch; burts** |
| sweet pepper | **k'oa yotsu burch** |
| rice | **duga** |
| salad | **salat** |
| salt | **tükha** |
| sandwich | **sendvich** |
| soup | **chorpa** |
| sugar | **sheekar** |
| candy | **konfeta; merza huma** |
| vinegar | **uksus** |
| yoghurt | **yettan shura** |

## VEGETABLES

| | |
|---|---|
| beetroot | **burak** |
| cucumber | **närs** |
| potato | **kartol(g)** |
| tomato | **pomidor** |
| vegetables | **khasstöömash** |

## FRUIT

| | |
|---|---|
| apple | ꜥazh |
| grape | kemsash |
| lemon | limon |
| melon | pasta |
| orange | apelsin |
| peach | ghammagha |
| plum | h'ach |
| sour plum | müsta h'ach |
| strawberry | ts'azamash |
| wild strawberry | toola |
| watermelon | horbaz |

## MEAT

| | |
|---|---|
| beef | bezhanan zhizhig |
| chicken | kootam |
| fish | ch'aara |
| lamb | ꜥaakhar |
| meat | zhizhig |
| pork | khaqi(n) zhizhig |
| sausage | yoh'; kolbasa |

## DRINK

Remember to ask for modern soft drinks by brand name.
Oh, and there's no real word for 'cheers'!

| | |
|---|---|
| alcohol | alkogol |
| bottle | shisha |
| brandy | konyak |
| can | banka |
| coffee | q'akho; kofe |
|    coffee with milk | shura tökhna kofi |
| fruit juice | sok |
| ice | sha |
| milk | shura |
| mineral water | mineralni khi |

| tea | **chai** |
|---|---|
|    tea with lemon |    **limon tesna chai** |
|    tea with milk |    **shura tökhna chai** |
|    no sugar, please |    **sheekar ma tooghlah'** |
| vodka | **q'arq'a** |
| whisky | **viski** |
| wine | **vino** |

## MORE ON FOOD & DRINK

Chechen cooking is delicious and has its own distinctive character. Starters include **Yu'ah'**, home-made sausage, and **B<sup>c</sup>ar** (literally: 'walnut'), which is a kind of boiled haggis served with rice and garlic sauce.

**Siskal** is a corn-flour bread eaten with meals. When served with **K'aldett** (more properly: **K'aldi Dett**), a cottage cheese dip with melted butter, it makes a delicious starter.

For main courses, try **Zhizhig Galnash** – stewed beef served up with garlic sauce and pasta. **K'ootam Galnash** uses chicken instead, and is served with pasta, roast onions with cream and butter.

**Ch'ee Palgash** are pastry pizzas filled cottage cheese, egg and onion, baked and then served up covered with melted butter.

**Maantesh** are similar to Chinese dumplings. Known as 'khinkal' in other parts of the Caucasus, the dumplings are stuffed with steamed minced lamb and herbs – eaten piping hot, they are the perfect remedy for a tired traveller.

**Chai**, or tea, is always served after meals.

## 9. DIRECTIONS

| | |
|---|---|
| Where is . . .? | . . . michah' wu/yu/du/bu*? |
| the art gallery | galerei (yu) |
| a bank | bank (yu) |
| the church | kils (yu) |
| the Ministry of . . . | . . . ministerstvo (yu) |
| the mosque | mäzhdig (du) |
| the city center | ghalii yuqqa (yu) |
| the . . . embassy | . . . posol'stvo (yu) |
| my hotel | sa gostinitsa (yu) |
| the market | baazar (yu) |
| the museum | muzei (yu) |
| the police | militsi (yu) |
| the post office | pochta (yu) |
| a toilet | h'oshtagh; tualet (yu) |
| the consulate | konsulstvo (yu) |
| the telephone center | telefon tsentr (yu) |
| an information office | spravochni (yu) |
| parliament | parlament (yu) |
| main square | ghalii(n) yuqqa (yu) |
| university | universitet (yu) |
| airport | aeroport (yu) |
| station | stantsi (yu) |
| academy | akademi (yu) |

| | |
|---|---|
| What . . . is this? | I . . . hu wu/yu/bu/du*? |
| bridge | t'ai (du) |
| building | ghishlo; ts'eno (du) |
| district | rayon (yu) |
| river | khi (du) |
| road | neq' (bu) |
| street | uuram (bu) |
| suburb | rayon (yu) |
| town | ghala (yu) |
| village | yurt (yu) |

* Depending on 'class' of thing referred – see page 8.

| | |
|---|---|
| What is this building? | **Otsu ts'eno choh' hu yu?** |
| What is that building? | **Iza hu ts'eno du?** |
| What time does it open? | **H'a mass dälcha yelloo iza?** |
| What time does it close? | **Dh'a mass dälcha q'owlalo iza?** |
| | |
| Can I park here? | **Quzah' mashen ghottoa megar dui?** |
| Are we on the right road for ...? | **... böducha nowq'ah' dui tkho?** |
| How many kilometers is it to ...? | **... qachallatsa mas kilometar yu?** |
| It is ... kilometers away. | **Quzar ... kilometar yu.** |
| How far is the next village? | **Qul t'iah' yolu yurt mel geena yu?** |
| Where can I find this address? | **Hoqa adres t'iah' yolu mettig michah' karor yar suna?** |
| Can you show me (on the map)? | **Karte t'iah' goitur yeri ah'?** |
| How do I get to ...? | **...-e mogha qochar war so?** |
| I want to go to ... | **So ... wagha lä'a?** |
| Can I walk there? | **So ghash t'e qoocha chah' yui 'iz?** |
| Is it far? | **Iza geenah' yui?** |
| Is it near? | **Iza 'ulläh' yui** |
| Is it far from/near here? | **Iz quzar genah'/ullyah' yui/dui/wui*?** |
| It is not far. | **Iza geenah' yats.** |
| Go straight ahead. | **Niisa dh'a gho.** |
| It's two blocks down. | **Iza shi kvartal oh'a waghacha yu.** |
| | |
| Turn left. | **Ättoo 'aaghor verza.** |
| Turn right. | **Ärroo 'aaghor verza.** |
| at the next corner | **sholghacha mä<sup>c</sup>niah'** |
| at the traffic lights | **svetofor yolchah'** |

\* Depending on 'class' of thing referred – see page 8.

| | |
|---|---|
| behind | **t'eh'a** |
| far | **geena** |
| in front of | **h'algha** |
| left | **ärroo 'aagho** |
| near | **ullee** |
| opposite | **döhh'al** |
| right | **ättoo 'aagho** |
| straight on | **niis dh'a** |
| | |
| bridge | **t'ai** |
| corner | **mä<sup>c</sup>ig; sa** |
| crossroads | **perekröstok; galmorze** |
| one-way street | **ts'h'an aaghorna böödu** |
| | **'uuram** |
| | |
| north | **q'ilbasiidi; sever** |
| south | **q'ilbi; yug** |
| east | **malkhbaali; vostok** |
| west | **malkhbuzi; zapad** |

# 10. SHOPPING

| | |
|---|---|
| Where can I find a . . . ? | **Suuna . . . michah' karor yar/ war/dar/bar*?** |
| Where can I buy . . . ? | **As . . . michah' öötsar yar/ war/dar/bar*?** |
| Where's the market? | **Baazar michah' yu?** |
| Where's the nearest . . . . ? | **Ulläh' yolu/dolu/bolu/wolu* . . . michah' yu/du/bu/wu*?** |
| Can you help me? | **Ts'h'a huma 'eera dari ah'.** |
| (Note: Can you rescue me? | **Suuna gho diira dari ah'.**) |
| Can I help you? | **Söögar nowq'ostal ööshi h'una?** |
| I'm just looking. | **So hozhush wu/yu.** |
| I'd like to buy . . . | **Suuna . . . eetsa lä'a.** |
| Could you show me some . . . ? | **. . . goitara yari/dari/bari* ah'?** |
| Can I look at it? | **Tsünga hazha megar dui?** |
| Do you have any . . . ? | **. . . yui/dui/bui* shügah'?** |
| This. | **Hara.** |
| That. | **D<sup>c</sup>aaranig.** |
| I don't like it. | **Iza suuna khaza tsa kheeta.** |
| I like it. | **Suuna 'iza yeeza.** |
| Do you have anything cheaper? | **Qul yoorakh qi humma yui shügah'?** |
| cheaper/better | **tsul yoorakh/tsul dika** |
| larger/smaller | **tsul yoqqa/tsul zhima** |
| Do you have anything else? | **Qi humma yui shügah'?** |
| Do you have any others? | **Qinarsh yui shügah'?** |
| Sorry, this is the only one. | **Bekhk ma billalah', har i bee qi yats.** |
| I'll take it. | **As iza s'h'a öötsu.** |
| How much/many do you want? | **Mel yeeza h'uuna?** |
| How much is it? | **Otsünakh hu döögha?** |

* Depending on 'class' of thing referred – see page 8.

| | |
|---|---|
| Can you write down the price? | **Tsüna makh dh'a yaazdeeh'?** |
| Could you lower the price? | **Makh oh' boqqar bari ah'?** |
| I don't have much money. | **Söögah' qi duqa akhcha a dats.** |
| Do you take credit cards? | **Kreditni kartochka dh'a öötsi ash?** |
| Would you like it wrapped? | **Dh'a h'archa yoi?** |
| Will that be all? | **Qi humma yui?** |
| Thank you, goodbye. | **Barkal h'una. ᶜA dika yoila.** |
| I want to return this. | **Hara yukha yala lä'ar suuna.** |
| | |
| auto spares store | **mashenan zapchastesh yukhku tüka** |
| baker's | **pekarni; bepig dottu mettig** |
| bank | **bank** |
| barber's | **parikmakherski; mesash khaado mettig** |
| I want a haircut please. | **San mesash dh'a khaada yeeh'a.** |
| bookshop | **knizhni tüka** |
| butcher's | **zhizhig dukhk mettig** |
| | |
| pharmacy | **apteka** |
| clothes store | **t'e yoogh human tüka** |
| dairy | **shurekh iina humanash; mashanan tüka** |
| dentist | **tsergii(n) lor** |
| department store | **univermag, yoqqa tüka** |
| dressmaker | **humanash tögurg** |
| electrical goods store | **elektrotovarsh dukhka tüka** |
| florist | **zezagash dukhkurg** |
| greengrocer | **ovoshnoi tüka** |
| hairdresser | **parikmakher** |
| hardware store | **khozyaistvenni tüka** |
| hospital | **bolnitsa** |

| | |
|---|---|
| kiosk | **kiyosk** |
| laundry | **prachechni** |
| market | **baazar** |
| newsstand | **kantselyarski tüka** |
| shoeshop | **obuvnoi tüka** |
| shop | **tüka** |
| souvenir shop | **sowghatan tüka** |
| stationer's | **kantselyarski tüka** |
| supermarket | **supermarket** |
| travel agent | **biletan kassa** |
| vegetable shop | **ovoshnoi tüka** |
| watchmaker's | **sah't toodesh mettig** |

## GIFTS

**Arts & crafts** — Much of Chechnya's traditions was destroyed and lost in the 1944 deportations by the Soviets. The art of carpet making has survived in some parts of Chechnya, bordering with Daghestan. Silvercraft (**detu'a humnash**), in particular *niello*, used to be widespread, in the form of fine belts, decorative trays, ewers, coffee pots and beakers. In some areas you may still find examples of chain-mail armour, swords and daggers (**kinjal**), as well as a wide range of horse-related trappings.

One impressive example of traditional craft that has almost been lost is the **istang**, a great felt tapestry covered in decorative motifs. It is hung on the wall of the main room of a house.

Normally a selection of arts and crafts can be bought at 'salons' — official handicrafts galleries. Remember that it is technically illegal to take out of the country any Chechen antiquities unless accompanied by the relevant paperwork.

| | |
|---|---|
| box | **ghutaq** |
| bracelet | **braslet** |
| brooch | **broshka** |
| candlestick | **ch'uuramhottorg** |
| carpet | **kuuza** |
| chain | **zäi; z<sup>c</sup>e** *(in mountainous Chechnya)* |
| clock | **sah't** |

# SHOPPING

| | |
|---|---|
| copper | **ts'asta** |
| crystal | **ts'ena angali** |
| earrings | **lergakh ukhkarsh** |
| enamel | **emall; sir** |
| gold | **deshi** |
| handicraft | **küüga yina huma** |
| iron | **echig** |
| jade | **nifrit** |
| jewelry | **mekhala huma** |
| kilim | **zhim kuuza** |
| leather | **t'ärska** |
| metal | **metal** |
| modern | **vai(n) kheenan** |
| necklace | **ozhereli** |
| pottery | **qiira pkheeghash** |
| ring | **ch'ug** |
| rosary | **sülkhanash** |
| silver | **deti** |
| steel | **bolat** |
| stone | **t'ulg** |
| traditional | **laamastan** |
| vase | **vaaza** |
| watch | **sah't** |
| wood | **dechig** |

## CLOTHES

Traditional Chechen costume takes on a variety of guises: from fiery First World War breeches and crimson jerkins to elegant black Valentino suits topped off by fedoras. Headgear is important in Chechen society, and apart from the fedoras there's quite an assortment on offer, including the big bell-shaped Astrakhan hat, made from soft karakul lambswool (**Nokhchi kui**), and the mink fur hat (**norki kui**). Sufis wear an unusual round tassled skull-cap, embroidered with silver thread.

| | |
|---|---|
| bag | **t'örmag** |
| belt | **dökhk** |

| | |
|---|---|
| boots | **etkash** |
| cotton | **(bamba) khlopok** |
| dress | **koch** |
| gloves | **kaarnash** |
| handbag | **zhima törmag** |
| hat | **kui** |
| jacket | **kastom** |
| jeans | **jinsesh** |
| leather | **t'ärska** |
| overcoat | **palto** |
| pocket | **kisa** |
| scarf | **gata; sharf** |
| shirt | **koch** |
| shoes | **maachash** |
| socks | **paastash** |
| suit | **kostüm** |
| sweater | **sviter** |
| tie | **galstuk** |
| trousers | **khecha** |
| umbrella | **zontik** |
| underwear | **chükhol yuugha humnash** |
| uniform | **forma** |
| wool | **t'argha** |

## TOILETRIES, ETC.

| | |
|---|---|
| aspirin | **aspirin** |
| bandaid | **bint; plastir** |
| comb | **yekhk** |
| condom | **preservativ** |
| cotton wool | **bamba** |
| deodorant | **dezodorant** |
| hairbrush | **schötka** |
| lipstick | **pomada** |
| mascara | **tush** |
| mouthwash | **baga khi qorzurg** |

# SHOPPING

| nail clippers | ma<sup>c</sup>arsh khado tukar |
|---|---|
| painkillers | analgin; lazar satsosh molkha; lazar teedesh molkha |
| perfume | dukhi |
| powder | pudar |
| razor | urs |
| razorblade | lezvesh |
| safety pin | halkha bullu maagha |
| shampoo | shampun |
| shaving cream | mazh yöösha krem |
| sleeping pills | nab qöötiit molkha |
| soap | saaba |
| sponge | gubka |
| sunscreen | malkhekh lardesh dolu krem |
| tampons | tamponash |
| thermometer | termometar |
| tissues | salfetkash |
| toilet paper | tualetan keekhat |
| toothbrush | tsergash yulu schötka |
| toothpaste | tsergash yulu pasta |

## STATIONERY

| ballpoint | shaarikovi ruchka |
|---|---|
| book | kinishka; kitaab; kniiga |
| dictionary | slovar |
| envelope | konvert |
| guidebook | neq'goiturg |
| ink | sheeq'a |
| magazine | zhurnal |
| map | karta |
| road map | neeq'an karta |
| a map of Grozny | Ghaliin karta |
| newspaper | gazet |
| a newspaper in English | ingals mottah' dolu gazet |
| notebook | zapisnoi knizhka |

| novels in English | **Ingals mottah' yaaziina romanash** |
| (piece of) paper | **keekhat** |
| pen | **q'oolam; ruchka** |
| pencil | **q'oolam; karandaash** |
| postcard | **otkritka** |
| scissors | **tukar** |
| writing paper | **keekhat** |

| Do you have any foreign publications? | **Qeecha pachkhalqeera gazetash dui shügah'?** |

## PHOTOGRAPHY

| How much is it to process this film? | **Plyonka yoqqarga hu döögha?** |
| When will it be ready? | **Iza matsa kiicha khira yu?** |
| I'd like a film for this camera. | **Hoqa foto aparatan plyonka yeezar suuna.** |
| B&W (film) | **cärzhi-k'ai** |
| camera | **foto aparat** |
| color (film) | **bos bolu plyonka** |
| film | **plyonka** |
| flash | **vspishka** |
| lens | **linza** |
| light meter | **eksponometr** |

## SMOKING

Cigarettes are usually purchased from kiosks. American brands are more pricey but still a bargain by western standards. Best value is buying by the carton and prices are normally fixed. It is also possible to buy cigarettes in singles. Chechens will smoke anywhere — it is rare indeed to find a smoke-free area and it is advisable to avoid constricted enclosed places if smoking creates problems for your health or if you simply find it offensive.

| A packet of cigarettes, please. | **Tsigärkan pachka looh'.** |

| | |
|---|---|
| Are these cigarettes strong/mild? | **Hara tsigärkash ch'oogha/ k'eeda yui?** |
| Do you have a light? | **Tsigärka latoo huma yui höögah'?** |
| Do you have any American cigarettes? | **Amerikanski tsigärkash yui shügah'?** |

| | |
|---|---|
| cigar | **sigar** |
| cigarette papers | **tsigärkan keekhat** |
| cigarettes | **tsigärkash** |
| a carton of cigarettes | **tsigärkan blok** |
| filtered | **filter yolu tsigärkash** |
| filterless | **filter yotsush tsigärkash** |
| flint | **kremenn; moqaz** |
| lighter fluid | **zazhigalkan benzin** |
| lighter | **zazhigalka** |
| matches | **sirnikash** |
| menthol | **mentol** |
| pipe | **lülla; trubka** |
| tobacco | **t'onka** |

## ELECTRICAL APPLIANCES

| | |
|---|---|
| adapter | **adapter** |
| battery | **batarei** |
| cd | **si-di; kompakt disk** |
| cd player | **kompakt disk player** |
| fan | **ventilyator** |
| hairdryer | **fen** |
| heating coil | **elektrobigudi** |
| iron (for clothing) | **itu** |
| kettle | **chaink** |
| plug | **vilka** |
| portable tv | **zhima televizor** |
| radio | **radiyo** |
| record | **plastinka** |
| tape (cassette) | **kaseta** |

| | |
|---|---|
| tape recorder | **magnitofon** |
| television | **televideni** |
| transformer | **transformator** |
| video (player) | **video-magnitofon** |
| videotape | **video-kaseta** |
| voltage regulator | **transformator** |

## SIZES

| | |
|---|---|
| small | **zhima** |
| big | **yoqqa** |
| heavy | **yeza** |
| light | **yay** |
| more | **duqa** |
| less | **kezzig** |
| too much/many | **duqa-duqa** |
| many | **duqa** |
| enough | **to'al** |
| that's enough | **tö'ar du** |
| also | **ishtta** |
| a little bit | **ts'h'a zhimma** |

| | |
|---|---|
| Do you have a carrier bag? | **Törmag bui shugah'?** |
| or | **Paket bui shugah'?** |

## 11. WHAT'S TO SEE

The Chechens have always been noted for their building and stone carving skills. The Soviets, however, systematically destroyed Chechen settlements and monuments in the wake of the 1944 deportations. Some have survived, although often they are difficult to get to.

With a former population of 400,000 but now devastated by war, Chechenya's only city Grozny (which means 'terrible' in Russian), or **Ghaala**, really dates from the frontier line from the days of Tsarist expansion. But every Chechen clan claims a town as its traditional center, each of which merits a visit. The word **aul** is used for villages and towns in the mountains while **yurt** tends to be used for those on the plains. The stone villages perched on rocky mountain sides can be stunning.

There too you can see the mysterious towers (**erza**) with their distinctive 'beehive' tops. Many of the cemeteries that still remain are impressive with their imposing headstones that can rise up to 8 ft high, beautifully carved in flowing Arabic characters. There are also still a few saints' shrines dotted about.

In the absence of any good guidebook, there is always the immense natural beauty of Chechnya, particularly the forests, teeming with wildlife (although many areas, sadly, are now heavily mined and therefore no-go areas), the racing rivers flowing from the glaciers and majestic snow-capped peaks.

Despite 200 years of pollution, destruction and invasion the Chechens still have good reason to be proud of their land.

| | |
|---|---|
| Do you have a guide-book/local map? | **Shügah' putevoditel yui/ karta dui?** |
| Is there a guide who speaks English? | **Ingals mott khu'ush gid wui quzah'?** |
| What are the main attractions? | **H'azha megar yolush mettagash hu yu?** |
| What is that? | **Iza hu yu?** |
| How old is it? | **Iza hu khan yolush yu?** |
| May I take a photograph? | **Surt daqqa megar dui?** |
| What time does it open/close? | **Iza mass dälcha s'h'a yelloo/ dh'a q'owla?** |

| | |
|---|---|
| What is this monument? | **Iza hu pamyatnik yu?** |
| What does that say? | **I boghurg hu du?** |
| Who is that statue of? | **Iza h'eena pamyatnik yu?** |
| Is there an entrance fee? | **Chu vödurg hu makh bala beeza?** |
| How much? | **Hu döögha?** |
| Are there any night clubs? | **Nochnoi klubash yui quzah'?** |
| Where can I hear local folk music? | **Nokhchi illeshka la doogha mettag yui quzah'?** |
| How much does it cost to get in? | **Chu vöödarg hu döögha?** |
| What's there to do in the evenings? | **Sarah' sa muq'a daqqa wagha mettaq yui?** |
| Is there a concert? | **Kontsert yui tsu chöah'?** |
| When is the wedding? | **Lowzarg matsa du?** |
| What time does it begin? | **Mas dälcha yolalo?** |
| Can we swim here? | **Liicha megar du quzah'?** |

| | |
|---|---|
| dancing | **khalkhar** |
| disco | **diskoteka** |
| disk-jockey | **disk-jokei** |
| exhibition | **vistavka** |
| folk dancing | **Nokhchi khalkhar** |
| folk music | **Nokhchi muzik; q'ooman muzik** |
| jazz | **jaz** |
| party | **sinq'eeram** |
| rock'n'roll | **rok** |
| blues | **bluuz** |

## BUILDINGS

| | |
|---|---|
| academy of sciences | **ᶜilmaniin akademi** |
| apartment | **kvartira** |
| archaeological | **arkheologicheski** |
| art gallery | **muzei** |
| bakery | **pekarni** |

| | |
|---|---|
| bar | **bar** |
| apartment block | **kvartiran ts'eeno** |
| building | **ghishloo; ts'eeno** |
| casino | **kazino** |
| castle | **ghaala** |
| cemetery | **keshnash** |
| church | **kilsa** |
| cinema | **kinoteatr** |
| city-map | **ghaalin karta** |
| college | **kollej** |
| concert hall | **kontsertan zal; kontsertni zal** |
| concert | **kontsert** |
| elevator | **lift** |
| embassy | **posolistvo** |
| hospital | **bolnitsi** |
| house | **ts'eeno** |
| housing project | **kvartiriin tsa** |
| library | **biblyoteka** |
| madrasa | **hüzhar; madrasa** |
| main square | **körta maidan** |
| market | **baazar** |
| monastery | **monastir** |
| monument | **pamyatnik** |
| mosque | **mäzhdig** |
| museum | **muzei** |
| nightclub | **nochnoi klub** |
| old city | **tisha ghala** |
| opera house | **opera** |
| park | **park** |
| parliament building | **parlamentan ghishlo** |
| restaurant | **restoran** |
| ruins | **sälnash** |
| saint's tomb | **ewlyaa'an kash** |
| 'salon' shop | **salon** |
| school | **ishkol** |
| shop | **tüka** |

| | |
|---|---|
| shrine | **ziyaart** |
| stadium | **stadyon** |
| statue | **statuya** |
| synagogue | **sinagoga** |
| temple | **ghishlo** |
| theatre | **teatar** |
| tomb | **kash** |
| tower | **t'eek'al dina tsa** |
| university | **universitet** |
| zoo | **zoopark** |

## OCCASIONS

| | |
|---|---|
| birth | **beera dar** |
| death | **valar** |
| funeral | **tezet** |
| marriage | **zud yaal yar\*** |

## RELIGIOUS HERITAGE

**Sufism** – Many Chechens are Sufis, followers of the mystical side of Islam. There are two **tariiqas** or paths – the Naqshbandi, historically based in the north, and the Qadiri, historically in the south. These are split up into between 70 and 80 smaller groupings. If you see Sufis performing the **zikr** – singing, dancing and banging drums – at festivals, then they will be Qadiris. A Qadiri follower is known as **h'azhi wird** (literally: 'hajj prayer'), while a Naqshbandi is known as **q'aili zikr** (literally: 'hidden holy-dance'). A Sufi in general will be called a **mürd**.

**Holidays & festivals** – There are a wide variety of traditional festivals celebrated in every village and area. Important dates in the national calendar are **Markhiin Butta** (Ramadan), **Ghurban <sup>c</sup>iid** (Id al-Adha) and **Markha Dostu <sup>c</sup>iid** (Id al-Fitr). A popular festival is the **Mawlid**, originating from a celebration in verse and song of the Prophet Muhammad's birthday, and now used as a vibrant means of celebrating events of significance to the community.

\* Literally: 'to take a wife.'

# 12. FINANCE

**Currencies** — The official currency in Chechnya is still the Russian rouble. Unofficially in use, but accepted everywhere outside of government establishments and retail outlets, are U.S. dollars. These may be refused however if notes are creased, torn, old, or simply a low denomination. Be prepared to accept change in roubles.

**Changing money** — In the absence of a reliable banking system, money is best changed in any bureau de change, where you will find reliable, up-to-date exchange rates prominently displayed on a board. The cashiers will often know a European language or two, and almost all will show the workings of the exchange on a calculator for you. Many shops and kiosks will also be happy to change money for you.

| | |
|---|---|
| I want to change some dollars. | **Suuna dollarsh kheetsa lä'ar.** |
| I want to change some pounds. | **Suuna funtash kheetsa lä'ar.** |
| Where can I change some money? | **Akhcha michah' kheetsa lur dar sööga?** |
| What is the exchange rate? | **Akhcha seenakh khöötsa ash?** |
| What is the commission? | **Akhcha khötsurg hu döögha?** |
| Could you please check that again? | **Yukha'a niisa dui h'azha?** |

| | |
|---|---|
| dollar | **dollar** |
| franc | **frank** |
| mark | **mark** |
| rouble | **som** |
| sterling | **funt sterling** |

| | |
|---|---|
| bank notes | **akhchan keekhatash** |
| calculator | **kalkulyator** |
| cashier | **kassa** |
| coins | **akhcha** |
| credit card | **kreditni karta** |

| commission | **komisiyonii; akhcha khötsurg lush bolu makh** |
| exchange | **akhcha khiitsar** |
| loose change | **meloch** |
| signature | **küg yazdara** |

## SOCIAL ORGANIZATION

**Family** – Chechens place great value on social bonds. Everybody traditionally belongs to one of approximately 130 **teips** or clans, which are divided into nine larger regional groupings called **tuqums**.

Chechen society teaches respect for tradition and one's elders. This has been carried over into the active mechanism of authority. Chechens turn to their elders for all major decisions, embodying as they do one of the three pillars of family, tradition and religion on which the nation has been built and which has helped it survive against all odds.

The village elders are the **baqqi-nakh** ('elder-men'), and include the <sup>c</sup>**ailem-nakh** ('people of knowledge' c ulema), the **yurt-qaid\*** ('qadi' or Muslim judge), the **yurt-muall** ('mullah' or Muslim clergyman), and the secular **yurt-da** ('father of the village' or mayor/official head of administration).

**Law** – The concept of law reflects this mixture. Normal law in the sense of law and order is **nizam**, while an individual law is called a **zakon**. Chechens also appeal to **shari<sup>c</sup>a**, Islamic law, or <sup>c</sup>**adat**, customary law or the law of their forefathers.

---

\* **Yurt** is used in this and the following terms even when the village is an **aul**!

## 13. COMMUNICATIONS

**Telecommunications** — When Chechnya's telephone system is connected up, all local calls are free although you need to use tokens in public phones. International calls are dialed direct, or else booked through the international operator, although this may incur a wait of several hours. Phones give one long ring to indicate a local call, two shorter rings for an international call. Satellite telephone links are costly but represent the only reliable and secure method of communication in and out of the area.

**Post office and communications** — When operational, the postal service in Chechnya is not always reliable. For important messages it would be best to stick to fax, telex, the telephone, couriers or e-mail. If you expect to receive mail, have it sent to the nearest headquarters of a host organization in another republic.

### AT THE POST OFFICE

| | |
|---|---|
| Where is the post office? | **Pochta michah' yu?** |
| What time does the post office open? | **Pochta mas dälcha s'h'a yellalo?** |
| What time does the post office close? | **Pochta mas dälcha dh'a q'owlalo?** |
| Where is the mail box? | **Pochtan yashka michah' yu?** |
| Is there any mail for me? | **Sa tserakh tesna ts'ha khekhat dui?** |
| | |
| How long will it take for this to get there? | **Hara quzar tsig dh'a qaachaltsa mel khan yeera yu?** |
| How much does it cost to send this to . . .? | **Hara . . . yoh'iiturg hu döögha?** |
| I would like some stamps. | **Suuna markanash yeezar.** |
| I would like to send . . . | **Suuna . . . tas lä'ara.** |
| a letter | **keekhat** |
| a postcard | **otkritka** |
| a parcel | **posilka** |
| a telegram | **telegrama** |

| air mail | aviya poshta |
| envelope | konvert |
| mailbox | poshtovi yashka |
| parcel | posilka |
| registered mail | zakaznoi poshta |
| stamp | marka; poshtan marka |
| telegram | telegrama |

## TELEPHONING

| Where is the telephone? | Telefon michah' yu? |
| May I use your phone? | Telefon tookha megar dui? |
| Can I telephone from here? | Quzar telefon tookha megar dui? |
| Can you help me get this number? | Hara nomer yolush bolcha naakhe telefon tookha ghodir dari ah'? |
| I would like to make a phone call. | Telefon tookha lä'ar suuna. |
| I would like to send a fax. | Faks tasa lä'ar suuna. |
| I would like to send a telex. | Teleks tasa lä'ar suuna. |
| I want to ring. . . | Suuna . . . telefon toogha lä'ar. |
| What is the code   for. . .? | . . . kod hu yu? |
| What is the international code? | Mezhdunarodni kod hu yu? |
| The number is . . . | Tsüna nomer . . . yu. |
| The extension is . . . | Dopolnitelni nomer . . . yu. |
| It's busy. | Linii muq'a yats. |
| *or* | Linii zaniati yu. |
| I've been cut off. | So q'amel desh lättashyah' hara dh'a yeelara. |
| The lines have been cut. | Linii dh'a khädda. |
| Can you help me get this number? | Hara telefon nomer tookha gho diira dari ah'? |
| Can I dial direct? | Operator vootsush telefon tookha lur yui sööga? |

| | |
|---|---|
| Where is the nearest public phone? | **Quz ulläh' telefon yui?** |
| I would like to speak to Mr./Mrs./Ms. . . . | **. . . -iga q'amel da megar dari?** |
| Can I leave a message? | **Zapiska iita megar dui?** |
| | |
| fax | **faks** |
| e-mail | **e-mail; elektroni pochta** |
| international operator | **mezhdunarodni operator** |
| Internet | **Internet** |
| modem | **modem** |
| operator | **operator** |
| satellite phone | **sputnikan telefon** |
| telex | **teleks** |

# 14. THE OFFICE

| | |
|---|---|
| chair | **ghant** |
| computer | **kompyutor** |
| desk | **stol** |
| drawer | **ghutaq** |
| fax | **faks** |
| file | **papka** |
| meeting | **vowshakhqeetar** |
| paper | **keekhat** |
| pen | **ruchka** |
| pencil | **q'oolam** |
| photocopier | **kseroks** |
| printer | **printer** |
| report | **doklad** |
| ruler | **lineika** |
| telephone | **telefon** |
| telex | **teleks** |
| typewriter | **pechatni mashen** |

## 15. THE CONFERENCE

| | |
|---|---|
| a break for refreshments | **sada<sup>c</sup>ar** |
| conference room | **konferentsi chöö** |
| copy | **kopi** |
| discussion | **diitsar dillar** |
| guest speaker | **qeiqin ve'ana dokladkho** |
| a paper | **keekhat** |
| podium | **tribuna** |
| projector | **proyektor** |
| a session chaired by . . . | **zasedani predsedatel . . . wu/yu.** |
| speaker | **dokladkho** |
| subject | **teema** |

# 16. THE FARM

| | |
|---|---|
| agriculture | **yurtan baakham** |
| barn | **bozhal** |
| cattle | **däh'nii** |
| to clear land | **ts'a(n) da** |
| combine harvester | **kombain** |
| corn | **h'äshk'a** |
| crops | **ooramat** |
| earth | **latta** |
| fallowland | **aakhar-latta** |
| farm | **ferma; baakham** |
| farmer | **aakharkho; fermer** |
| farming | **yurt baakham** |
| animal feed | **korm** |
| fertilizer | **udobreni** |
| field | **aaree; latta** |
| fruit | **stöömash** |
| garden | **khasbesh; ogorod** |
| to grow crops | **ooramatash leeloo** |
| harvest | **yaltash** |
| hay | **yol** |
| haystack | **yeelan khola** |
| marsh | **üshal** |
| mill | **h'eera** |
| orchard | **besh** |
| planting | **(ooramatash) dooghar** |
| plow | **goota** |
| to plow | **akha** |
| reaping | **k'a h'eegar** |
| season | **sizon** |
| seed | **hu** (*plural* **hush**) |
| sowing | **hush dh'a deer** |
| tractor | **traktor** |
| wheat | **k'a** |
| well (of water) | **ghu** |

## 17. ANIMALS

**MAMMALS**

| | |
|---|---|
| bear | cha |
| bull | stu |
| cat | tsitska |
| cow | yetta; h'aiba |
| deer | sai |
| dog | zh<sup>c</sup>ala |
| donkey | vir |
| flock | zha |
| goat | gaaza |
| herd | bazha |
| horse | gowra |
| lamb | <sup>c</sup>akhar |
| mare | qeela |
| mouse | dakhka |
| mule | b<sup>c</sup>arza |
| pig | häqa |
| pony | poni |
| rabbit | ph'aagal |
| ram | üstagh |
| rat | muq'a dakhka |
| sheep | zhii |
| sheepdog | zhen zh<sup>c</sup>ala |
| stallion | aighar |
| wolf | borz |

**Birds**

| | |
|---|---|
| bird | olkhazar |
| chicken/hen | kootam |
| rooster | n<sup>c</sup>ana |
| crow | q'ig |
| duck | badd |
| eagle | ärzu |
| goose | ghaz |

| | |
|---|---|
| owl | **buha** |
| partridge | **moosha** |
| turkey | **moskal** |

## INSECTS AND AMPHIBIANS

| | |
|---|---|
| ant | **zintak** |
| bee | **naqar moza** |
| butterfly | **polla** |
| caterpillar | **nᶜäwtsitsig** |
| cockroach | **chh'awrig** |
| fish | **ch'ᶜara** |
| flea | **sagal** |
| fleas | **segli** |
| fly | **moza** |
| frog | **pkhid** |
| insect | **sagalmat** |
| lizard | **mölq'a** |
| louse | **meza** |
| mosquito | **chürk** |
| snail | **etmäᶜig** |
| snake | **läh'a** |
| spider | **gezg** |
| termite | **termit** |
| tick | **vechchalg** |
| wasp | **zᶜüüga** |
| worm | **nᶜana** |

# 18. COUNTRYSIDE

| | |
|---|---|
| avalanche | h'ätta; laamanan h'ätta |
| canal | taatol |
| cave | h'ekh |
| copse | bölak |
| dam | sunt |
| earthquake | mokhk beegor |
| fire | ts'e |
| flood | khi t'edaalar |
| foothills | laaman k'aazha |
| foothpath | tacha |
| forest | h'un |
| hill | goo |
| lake | ᶜam |
| landslide | toqam |
| mountain | lam |
| mountain pass | duq' |
| peak | boh' |
| plain | aare |
| plant | ooramat |
| range | laamanan mogha |
| ravine | ch'ozh |
| river bank | khi yist |
| river | khi |
| rock | tarkh |
| slope | base |
| stream | taatol |
| summit | boh' |
| swamp | üshal |
| tree | ditt |
| valley | tooghee |
| waterfall | chukhchari |
| a wood | h'un |

## 19. THE WEATHER

In the plains in the northern part of the country the winters are wet and the summers hot and sticky. In the forested foothills further south, all four seasons tend to be clearly defined, with brilliant springs, balmy summers, golden autumns and crisp winters. The southern mountain slopes have cool summers and harsh winters which result in some areas being snowed in for over half the year.

| | |
|---|---|
| What's the weather like? | **Pogoda moogha yu?** |
| *or* | **Aarah' moogha du?** |
| The weather is . . . today. | **Takhana pogoda . . . yu.** |
| *or* | **Takhana aarah' . . . yu.** |
| cold | **shiila** |
| cool/fresh | **shiila** |
| cloudy | **markhash yolu** |
| foggy | **dokhk dui** |
| freezing | **ghoriina** |
| hot | **yowkha** |
| misty | **dokhka** |
| very hot | **huno yowkha** |
| windy | **mokh bälla** |

| | |
|---|---|
| It is raining. | **Dogha doogha.** |
| It is snowing. | **Loo doogha.** |
| It is sunny. | **Malkha häzhna de(n) du.** |

| | |
|---|---|
| air | **hawa'** |
| cloud | **markha; qöölana** |
| fog | **dokhk** |
| frost | **shiilo** |
| full moon | **butt buzar** |
| heatwave | **yowkho** |
| ice | **sha** |
| midsummer | **äkhke yuqqa** |
| midwinter | **ᶜa(n) yuqqe** |
| mild winter | **k'eeda ᶜa(n)** |

| | |
|---|---|
| moon | **butt** |
| new moon | **butt ts'inbaalar** |
| rain | **dogha** |
| severe winter | **wunoo shiila <sup>c</sup>a(n)** |
| sleet | **deshash dolu loo** |
| snow | **loo** |
| solstice | **malkh ts'a qachar** |
| star | **seeda** |
| sun | **malkh** |
| sunny | **malkh qetta** |
| thaw | **yashar** |
| weather | **pogoda; khena hottam** |
| wind | **mokh** |

## SEASONS

| | |
|---|---|
| spring | **b<sup>c</sup>ästee** |
| summer | **äkhkee** |
| autumn | **güiree** |
| winter | **<sup>c</sup>a; <sup>c</sup>an** |

## 20. CAMPING

| | |
|---|---|
| Where can we camp? | **Laager tökhna sowtsa michah' megar du?** |
| Can we camp here? | **Quzah' palatka ghotto megar dui?** |
| Is it safe to camp here? | **Qeeram botsush palatka ghotto mettag yui h'ar?** |
| Is there drinking water? | **Molu khi dui quzah'?** |
| May we light a fire? | **Ts'e latoo megar dui ookh?** |

| | |
|---|---|
| axe | **dig** |
| backpack | **rügzak** |
| bucket | **chiilik; vedar** |
| campsite | **laager tuukha mettig** |
| can opener | **otkrivalka** |
| compass | **kompas** |
| firewood | **daago dechig** |
| flashlight | **stogar; fonarik** |
| gas canister | **gaz balon** |
| hammer | **zh<sup>c</sup>ow** |
| ice axe | **sha boogho dig** |
| lamp | **stogar** |
| mattress | **göö** |
| penknife | **moqa; zhim urs** |
| rope | **tiirag** |
| sleeping bag | **vüzhu gali; spalni meshok** |
| stove | **pesh** |
| tent | **palatka** |
| tent pegs | **palatkiiin h'öqanash** |
| water bottle | **khin shisha** |

## 21. IN CASE OF EMERGENCY

**Complaining** — If you really feel you have been cheated or misled, raise the matter first with your host or the proprietor of the establishment in question — preferably with a smile. Chechens are proud but courteous, with a deeply felt tradition of hospitality, and they consider it their duty to help any guest. Angry glares and shouting will get you nowhere.

**Crime** — Chechens are generally law-abiding people, but petty theft does occur. Without undue paranoia, take usual precautions. If you are robbed, contact the police. Of course in the more remote areas, sensible precautions should be taken, and always ensure that you go with a guide. In general, follow the same rules as you would in your own country and you will run little risk of encountering crime.

**Disabled facilities** — The terrain and conditions throughout most of Chechnya do not make it easy for any visitor to get around in a wheelchair even at the best of times. Access to most buildings in Grozny and the towns is difficult, particularly since the majority of lifts do not function. Facilities are rarely available in hotels, the airport or other public areas.

**Toilets** — You will find public utilities located in any important or official building. You may use those in hotels or restaurants. You will often encounter failed plumbing and absence of toilet paper.

| | |
|---|---|
| Help! | **Gho daish!** |
| Could you help me please? | **Suuna gho deeh'?** |

| | |
|---|---|
| Do you have a telephone? | **Telefon yui shügah'?** |
| Can I use your telephone? | **As telefon toogha megar dui?** |
| Where is the nearest telephone? | **Ulläh' telefon yolu mettig michah' yu?** |
| Does the phone work? | **Telefon bolkh besh yui?** |
| Get help quickly! | **Gho qeiqalah' sekh!** |

| | |
|---|---|
| Call the police. | **Militsi qeiqa.** |
| I'll call the police! | **As militsig qöiqh'uuna!** |

| | |
|---|---|
| Is there a doctor near here? | **Quz ulläh' lor wui?** |

| | |
|---|---|
| Call a doctor. | **Lööri qeiqa.** |
| Call an ambulance. | **Skori pomosh qeiqa.** |
| I'll get medical help! | **As lor waalor wu!** |

| | |
|---|---|
| Where is the doctor? | **Lor michah' wu?** |
| Where is the hospital? | **Bolnitsi michah' yu ?** |
| Where is the chemist? | **Apteka michah' yu ?** |
| Where is the dentist? | **Tsergin lor michah' wu ?** |
| Where is the police station? | **Militsi otdel michah' yu?** |

| | | |
|---|---|---|
| There's been an accident! | | **Avari khilla** |
| Is anyone hurt? | | **Stagga'a laziini?** |
| This person is hurt. | | **Hara stag laza vina wu.** |
| There are people injured. | | **Nakh laziina quzah'.** |
| Don't move! | *to a male* | **Mettakh ma waalalah'!** |
| | *to a female* | **Mettakh ma yaalalah'!** |
| Go away! | *to a male* | **Dh'a waalah' quzar!** |
| | *to a female* | **Dh'a yaalah' quzar!** |
| | *to a group* | **Dh'a dowliish quzar!** |

| | |
|---|---|
| I am lost. | **So tilla.** |
| I am ill. | **So tsomgash wu/yu.** |
| I've been raped. | **So hiiza iina.** |
| Take me to a doctor. | **Lor volcha vigah' so.** |

| | |
|---|---|
| I've been robbed. | **Söögar humnash dh'a yaghna.** |
| Thief! | **Q'u!** |
| My . . . has been stolen. | **Sa . . . lach'qa iina.** |
| I have lost my . . . | **As sai . . .** |
|     my bags |     **t'örmag bai'ana** |
|     my camera equipment |     **kamiritsa bolu ghirsa bai'ana** |
|     my handbag |     **zhima t'örmag bai'ana** |
|     my laptop computer |     **zhima kompütor** |
|     my money |     **akhcha dai'ana** |

| | |
|---|---|
| my passport | **pasport dai'ana** |
| my sound equipment | **zuvkovoi ghirsa bai'ana** |
| my travelers' checks | **dorozhni cheekash yai'ana** |
| my wallet | **bokhcha dai'ana.** |
| My possessions are insured. | **Sa humnash strakhovka yollush yu.** |
| I have a problem. | **Ts'h'a problema yar sa.** |
| I didn't do it. | **Iza as tsa dina.** |
| I'm sorry. | **Bekhk ma billalah'.** |
| I apologize. _to a male_ | **Q'in t'eera waalalah' suuna.** |
| _to a female_ | **Q'in t'eera yaalalah' suuna.** |
| I didn't realize anything was wrong. | **Suuna söögar ghaalat dälleer tsa kha'ar.** |
| I want to contact my embassy. | **So sai posolstvekh q'eeta veeza/yeeza.** |
| I want to contact my consulate. | **So sai konsulstvekh q'eeta veeza/yeeza.** |
| I speak English. | **As Ingalsi motta büütsa.** |
| I need an interpreter. | **Suuna perevodchik öösha.** |
| Where are the toilets? | **H'oshtagh/Tualet michah' yu?** |
| clinic | **klinika** |
| doctor | **lor** |
| nurse | **loryisha; medsestra** |
| hospital | **bolnitsi** |
| policeman | **militsiyoner** |
| police | **militsi** |
| police station | **militsi otdel** |

## 22. HEALTHCARE

**Health/medical information** — Make sure any insurance policy you take out covers Chechnya, although this will only help in flying you out in case of a serious accident or illness. No vaccinations are required for Chechnya, although your doctor may suggest you take the boosters usually recommended when making any trip outside of North America and Western Europe.

**Chemists** are easy to find but tend to be chronically understocked or simply empty even in peacetime. It is probably best to bring a sufficient supply of any medication you require — even basics such as aspirin, cotton wool or sunscreen.

| | |
|---|---|
| What's the trouble? | **Hu khilla?** |
| I am sick. | **So tsomgush wu/yu.** |
| My companion is sick. | **Sa naaq'ost tsomgush wu/yu.** |
| May I see a female doctor? | **Ste lor ga megar dari?** |
| I have medical insurance. | **Söögah' meditsinksi trakhovka yu.** |
| Please undress. | **Hain t'eera humnash dh'a yaaghah'.** |

### AILMENTS

| | |
|---|---|
| How long have you had this problem? | **I tsomgar h'a dolu mel khan yu?** |
| How long have you been feeling sick? | **Ho tsomgush volu/yolu mel khan yu?** |
| Where does it hurt? | **Michah' laza?** |
| It hurts here. | **Quzah' laza.** |
| I have been vomiting. | **So ᶜätta vina/yina.** |
| I feel dizzy. | **Suuna bh'aagor h'iiza.** |
| I can't eat. | **Sööga huma tsa ya'lo.** |
| I can't sleep. | **Suuna nab tsa qeeta.** |
| I feel worse. | **Suuna vwo kheeta.** |
| I feel better. | **Suuna ghooliah' kheeta.** |

| I am . . . | Sa . . . |
| Are you . . .? | H'a . . .? |
| diabetic | diabet yu? |
| epileptic | epilepsi yu? |
| asthmatic | astma yu? |

| I'm pregnant. | So beerakh yu. |

| I have. . . | Sa . . . wu/yu/du/bu.* |
| You have . . . | H'a . . . wu/yu/du/bu.* |
| a temperature | daagar (du) |
| an allergy | allergii (yu) |
| an infection | infektsi (yu) |
| an itch | k'am dalar (du) |
| fever | daagar (du) |

| I have a cold. | So shell vella/yella. |
| You have a cold. | H'o shell vella/yella. |
| I have a cough. | Suuna yowkharsh qetta. |
| You have a cough. | H'uuna yowkharsh qetta. |

| I have a headache. | Sa kort laza. |
| I have toothache. | Sa tserg laza. |
| I have a sore throat. | Sa legash laza. |
| I have a stomachache. | Sa chöö laza. |
| I have a fracture. | Sa meezhee kag yina. |
| I have backache. | Suuna ann khöötta. |
| I have constipation. | Sa chöö yuq'a yalla. |
| I have diarrhea. | Suuna choh' lazar qetta. |

| I have a heart condition. | Sa dog ghiila du. |
| I have a pain in my heart. | Sa dog laza. |

## MEDICATION

| I take this medication. | As i molkha molu. |
| I need medication for. . . | Suuna . . .-na molkha deeza. |

* Depending on 'class' of thing referred – see page 8.

| | | |
|---|---|---|
| What type of medication is this? | | **Iza hu molkha du?** |
| How many times a day must I take it? | | **Diinah' massaz mala deza as i molkha?** |
| When should I stop? | | **So matsa satsa veeza/yeeza.** |
| I'm on antibiotics. | | **So antibiotikash molush wu/ yu.** |
| I'm allergic to . . . | | **Sa . . .-na alergii yu.** |
| antibiotics | | **antibiotikash** |
| penicillin | | **penitsilin** |
| I have been vaccinated. | | **So vaktsinan maakha töghna wu/yu.** |
| I have my own syringe. | | **Söögah' sai maakha bu.** |
| Is it possible for me to travel? | m | **Nowq'a waala megar dui suuna?** |
| | f | **Nowq'a yaala megar dui suuna?** |
| painkiller | | **lazar satsosh molkha** |
| tranquilizer | | **trankvilizator** |
| aspirin | | **aspirin** |
| antibiotic | | **antibiotiik** |
| drug | | **molkha** |

## HEALTH WORDS

| | |
|---|---|
| AIDS | **SPID** |
| alcoholic | **alkagolik** |
| alcoholism | **alkagolizm** |
| anemia | **anemia** |
| amputation | **meezhee dh'a yaqqar; amputatsi** |
| anesthetic | **anasteziiya** |
| anesthetist | **anastezist** |
| antibiotic | **antibiotik** |

| | |
|---|---|
| antiseptic | **chow dh'a yerzosh molkha; antiseptik** |
| blood | **ts'ii** |
| blood group | **ts'iina gruppa** |
| blood pressure: | |
| low blood pressure | **logha davleni** |
| high blood pressure | **leqa davleni** |
| blood transfusion | **ts'ii dottar** |
| bone | **däᶜakhk** |
| cancer | **rak** |
| cholera | **kholera** |
| clinic | **bolnitsa** |
| dentist | **tsergi(n) lor** |
| epidemic | **epidemi** |
| fever | **khorsha** |
| flu | **gripp** |
| fracture | **meezhee kagyar** |
| frostbite | **dah'a dar** |
| germs | **bakteresh** |
| heart attack | **infarkt** |
| hepatitis | **gipatit** |
| hygiene | **gigiyena** |
| indigestion | **yi'narg tsa laarlo** |
| infection | **infektsi** |
| influenza | **gripp** |
| limb | **meezhee** |
| needle | **maakha** |
| nurse | **medsestra** |
| operating theatre | **operatsiin zal** |
| (surgical) operation | **operatsi** |
| oxygen | **kislorod** |
| pain | **lazar** |
| physiotherapy | **fiziyoterapia** |
| pins and needles | **meekhi** |
| rabies | **h'eera woolu tsamgar** |
| shrapnel | **oskolkash** |

| | |
|---|---|
| snake bite | **läho katookhar** |
| stethoscope | **stetoskop** |
| stomachache | **kiira lazar** |
| surgeon | **lor, khirurg** |
| (act of) surgery | **operatsi** |
| syringe | **maakha** |
| thermometer | **termometar** |
| toothache | **tserg lazar** |
| torture | **stagan nitsqa ba(n)** |

## EYESIGHT

| | |
|---|---|
| I have broken my glasses. | **As sain küzganash dookiina.** |
| Can you repair them? | **Üsh taalur dari hööga?** |
| I need new lenses. | **Suuna kella küzganash deeza.** |
| When can I collect them? | **S'h'a 'eetsa matsa kiicha khir du 'üsh?** |
| How much do I owe you? | **Söögar hu makh bookha?** |
| | |
| contact lenses | **linzash** |
| contact lens solution | **linzash choh' latto rastvor** |

## 23. RELIEF AID

| | |
|---|---|
| Can you help me? | **Suuna gho diira dari ah'?** |
| Do you speak English? | **H'uuna Ingals mott biitsa kha'i?** |
| Who is in charge? | **Körtnig mil wu quzah'?** |
| Fetch the main person in charge. | **Häkam s'h'a vaala ve.** |
| What's the name of this town? | **Hara hu ghala yu?** |
| How many people live there? | **Mas adam du tsigah' deeghash?** |
| What's the name of that river? | **Iza hu khi du/otsu khin tse hu yu?** |
| How deep is it? | **Iza mel k'orga du?** |
| Is the bridge still standing? | **Tsun t'ökhal döödush t'ai hintsa lättash dui?** |
| What is the name of that mountain? | **Otsu looman tse hu yu?** |
| How high is it? | **Mel leqa bu iz?** |
| Where is the border? | **Dooza michah' du?** |
| Is it safe? | **Qeeramza dui iza?** |
| Show me. | **H'a gaita.** |

### CHECKPOINTS

| | |
|---|---|
| checkpoint | **post** |
| roadblock | **blokpost** |
| Stop! | **Satsiita!** |
| Do not move! | **Mettagha ma waala!** |
| Go! | **Dh'a ghoo!** |
| Who are you? | **H'o mil wu/yu?** |
| Don't shoot! | **Gerza ma tooghalah'!** |
| help! | **Gho daish!** |
| no entry | *Russian* **vkhoda nyet** |
| no admission | *Russian* **vkhod zapreshchyon** |
| emergency exit | *Russian* **avariinyi vykhod** |

| | |
|---|---|
| straight on | **niisa dh'a** |
| turn left | **ärroo 'aaghor verza/yerza** |
| turn right | **ättoo 'aaghor verza/yerza** |
| this way | **quzzagkhula** |
| that way | **d<sup>c</sup>agakhula** |
| Keep quiet! | **Ghowgha ma ye!** |
| You are right. | **H'o niisa löö.** |
| You are wrong. | **H'o khartsa löö.** |
| I am ready. | **So kiicha wu/yu.** |
| I am in a hurry. | **So sikha wu/yu.** |
| Well, thank you! *(in reply)* | **Barkalla!** |
| What's that? | **Iza hu du?** |
| Come in! | **Chööh'a waala/yaala!** |
| That's all! | **Qi humma dats!** |

### FOOD DISTRIBUTION

| | |
|---|---|
| This is a feeding station. | **Hara ya'a huma lush stantsi yu.** |
| How many people in your family? | **H'a döözalah' mas stag wu?** |
| How many children? | **Mas beera du?** |
| You must come back this afternoon. | **Delqa khan t'iah' yukha vaa veeza h'o.** |
| tonight | **tkhowsa** |
| tomorrow | **qaana** |
| the day after | **qaana <sup>c</sup>iicha** |
| next week | **k'ira dälcha** |
| There is water for you. | **Hara khi du h'uuna.** |
| There is grain for you. | **Hara k'a du h'uuna.** |
| There is food for you. | **Hara ya'a huma yu h'uuna.** |
| There is fuel for you. | **Hara benzin du h'uuna.** |

### ROAD REPAIR

| | |
|---|---|
| Is the road passable? | **Otsa neeq'akhola dh'a vöödila dui?** |
| Is the road blocked? | **Neq' q'oilanam bats?** |

| | |
|---|---|
| Are the bridges intact? | **T'aish huma khilaz dui?** |
| Are there any obstacles? | **Ts'h'aa döhaloonash yui tsigah'?** |
| What is it blocked with? | **Döhaloo yirg hu yu?** |
| holes? | **ornash?** |
| trees? | **dittash?** |
| rocks? | **tarkhnash?** |
| landslide? | **toqam?** |
| something else? | **q'i yolu huma?** |
| Are there any road-building machines nearby? | **Ts'h'aa neeq'ash toodesh masheenash yui quzah'?** |
| We are repairing the road. | **Tkho neq' toobesh du.** |
| We are repairing the bridge. | **Tkho t'ai toobesh du.** |
| We need . . . | **Tkhuuna . . . öösha.** |
| wood | **dechig** |
| rock | **tarkhanash** |
| gravel | **gravii** |
| sand | **ghum** |
| fuel | **benzin** |

## MINES

| | |
|---|---|
| mine *noun* | **miina** |
| mines | **miinash** |
| mine *adjective* | **miiniin** |
| minefield | **miiniin aare** |
| to lay mines | **miina yila** |
| to hit a mine | **miina t'iah' eqqar** |
| to clear a mine | **miina dh'a yaqqar** |
| mine detector | **miinash bilgal yookhush detektor** |
| mine disposal | **miinash zee naz ya** |
| Are there any mines near here? | **Quzah' gondah' miinash yui?** |
| What type are they? | **Mülkha taipa yu 'üsh?** |
| anti-vehicle | **protivotankovi** |

| | |
|---|---|
| anti-personnel | **protivopekhotni** |
| plastic | **plastikovi miina** |
| floating | **khi(n) t'iah' lelash yolu miina** |
| magnetic | **magnitni miina** |
| tripwire | **saargakh tesna yolu miina** |
| What size are they? | **Mülkha baaramäh' yu 'üsh?** |
| What color are they? | **Mülkha basäh' yu 'üsh?** |
| Are they marked? | **Bilgaliaghna yui 'üsh?** |
| How? | **Moogha?** |
| How many mines are there? | **Mas miina yu tsigah'?** |
| When were they laid? | **Üsh matsa yekhkaneera.** |
| Can you take me to the minefields? | **Minii aaree yolcha vügar vari ah' so?** |
| Are there any booby traps near there? | **Quzah' ts'h'aa guuranash yui?** |
| Are they made from grenades, high explosives or something else? | **Üsh granatekh ya vzvivchatkekh yina yu?** |
| Are they in a building? | **Üsh ts'eenoo choh' yui?** |
| on tracks? | **tachanash t'iah'?** |
| on roads? | **neeqash t'iah'?** |
| on bridges? | **t'aish t'iah'?** |
| or elsewhere? | **ya qeechanah'?** |
| Can you show me? | **Goitar yari ah' suuna 'üsh?** |

**OTHER WORDS**

| | |
|---|---|
| airforce | **VVS ('ve-ve-es')** |
| ambulance | **skori pomosh** |
| armored car | **BTR ('be-ve-er')** |
| army | **eskar; armi** |
| artillery | **artileri** |
| barbed wire | **q'okhtsal saara** |
| bomb | **bomba** |
| bomber | **bombardirovshik** |

| | |
|---|---|
| bullet | **d<sup>c</sup>ändarg** |
| cannon | **yoqqa top** |
| disaster | **bookham; katastrofa** |
| fighter | **istrebiteli** |
| gun | **top; yoq top** |
| machine gun | **avtomat** |
| missile | **rakeeta** |
| missiles | **raketash** |
| natural disaster | **<sup>c</sup>aalaman bookham** |
| navy | **VMS ('ve-em-es')** |
| officer | **ofitser; epsar** |
| parachute | **chetar; parashyut** |
| peace | **maashar** |
| people | **nakh** |
| pistol | **tapcha** |
| refugee camp | **boida neekha lager** |
| relief aid | **k'elh'aara vaqqar** |
| sack | **gali** |
| shell | **snaryad; kho'** |
| shrapnel | **oskwol kash** |
| tank | **tank** |
| troops | **salti** |
| unexploded bomb | **eqqaz yolu bomba** |
| United Nations | **O.O.N. ('o-on')** |
| war | **t'om** |

**REFUGEES**

The Russian word **bezhenets** (*plural* **bezhenetsash**) is used as the general word for refugee. Displaced Persons as a result of war are **(t'emua) tseera bäkhna nakh** ('people forced from their homes [in war]'). Someone who flees or escapes is called **veddarg/yeddarg** (*plural* **boidda**).

## 24. TOOLS

| | |
|---|---|
| binoculars | **binokal** |
| brick | **kibarchik** |
| brush | **shchötka** |
| butane canister | **gaz balon** |
| cable | **kabel; saarg** |
| cooker | **plita** |
| drill | **drel** |
| glasses, sunglasses | **küzganash** |
| hammer | **zhᶜow** |
| handle | **t'am** |
| hose | **shlang** |
| insecticide | **sagalmatash yoi'u molkha** |
| ladder | **laame** |
| machine | **mashen** |
| microscope | **mikroskop** |
| nail | **h'ostam** |
| padlock | **doogha** |
| paint | **basar** |
| pickaxe | **kirka** |
| plank | **uy** |
| plastic | **plastmass** |
| rope | **t'iirag** |
| rubber | **rezen** |
| rust | **meeqa** |
| saw | **kherkh** |
| scissors | **tukar** |
| screw | **shurup** |
| screwdriver | **otvertka** |
| spade | **bell** |
| spanner | **mashenan doogha** |
| string | **tiirag** |
| telescope | **teleskop** |
| varnish | **lak** |
| wire | **saarg** |

## 25. THE CAR

**Driving** — Unless you already know the country well, it is inadvisable to bring your own vehicle to Chechnya. If you do, you will need an international driver's license, car registration papers and insurance. It is unlikely you will find spare parts for any vehicle other than those made in the ex-USSR. Driving conditions used to be good, although the recent conflicts have taken their predictable toll on the road system. Roads used to be well marked. Street lighting is sporadic, and traffic lights, if they exist, rarely work. Certain areas have parking restrictions, although it is not always obvious where they are nor what the restrictions are. Rather than book you, the police will simply remove the license plates of an illegally parked car. The driver then has to discover which police unit or station is holding them, and negotiate a suitable fee for their return. The military, however, may not be so understanding.

| | |
|---|---|
| Where can I rent a car? | **Mashen prokaate lush mettag yui quzah'?** |
| Where can I rent a car with a driver? | **Shoför wolush mashen prokaate lush mettag yui quzah'?** |
| How much is it per day? | **Diinah' hu makh bal beeza?** |
| How much is it per week? | **K'irnah' hu makh bal beeza?** |
| Can I park here? | **Mashen quzah' yita megar dui?** |
| Are we on the right road for . . .? | **. . . böödu nowq'ah' dui tkho?** |
| Where is the nearest filling station? | **Quza ülleera zapravka michah' yu?** |
| Fill the tank please.<br>    normal/diesel | **Bak yuz yeh'.**<br>    **benzin/diizel** |
| Check the oil/tires/<br>battery, please. | **Dättanga/churgashka/<br>akumulyatorga h'azha.** |

| | |
|---|---|
| I've broken down. | **Sa mashen yoghna.** |
| I have a puncture. | **Sa churg iqqan.** |
| I have run out of gas. | **Sa(n) benzin qaachiin.** |
| Our car is stuck (in a ditch). | **Tkha mashen (orchu yakhna) setsa.** |
| There's something wrong with this car. | **Har mashen lartäh' yats.** |
| We need a mechanic. | **Tkhuuna mekhanik veeza.** |
| Where is the nearest garage? | **Quza 'ulläh' yolu tekh stantsi michah' yu?** |
| Can you tow us? | **Tkha mashen buksirtsa dh'a yugar yari ash?** |
| Can you jump start the car? | **Tettana lator yari ash mashen?** |
| There's been an accident. | **Quzah' avaari khillera.** |
| My car has been stolen. | **Sa mashen lachq'a yina.** |
| Call the police. | **Politsiiqa/Militsiiqa qeiqah'.** |
| | |
| driver's license | **pravaash** |
| insurance policy | **strakhovoi polis** |
| car papers | **tekh pasport** |
| car registration | **mashena(n) nomer** |

## WORDS

| | |
|---|---|
| accelerator | **gaz pedal** |
| air | **hawa'** |
| anti-freeze | **antifriz** |
| battery | **akumulyator** |
| bonnet | **kapot** |
| boot | **bagazhnik** |
| brake | **tormoz** |
| bumper | **bamper** |
| car park | **stoyanitka** |
| clutch | **stsepleni** |
| driver | **voditel** |
| engine | **motor** |

# THE CAR

| | |
|---|---|
| exhaust | **vikhlopnoi turb** |
| fan belt | **remen; motora(n) remen** |
| gear | **peredacha** |
| indicator light | **povorotnik** |
| inner-tube | **kamer** |
| jack | **domkrat** |
| mechanic | **mekhanik** |
| neutral drive | **neitralnyi** |
| oil | **dätta** |
| oilcan | **dätta(n) kanistar** |
| passenger | **pasazhir** |
| petrol | **benzin** |
| radiator | **radiyator** |
| reverse | **zadnyi skorost** |
| seat | **sideni** |
| spare tire | **zapaska** |
| speed | **skorost** |
| steering wheel | **rul** |
| tank | **bak** |
| tow rope | **buksiran mush; tiirag** |
| tyre | **churg** |
| windscreen | **h'alkhara küzg** |

# 26. COLORS

| | |
|---|---|
| black | <sup>c</sup>ärzha |
| blue | siina |
| brown | böömasha |
| green | bätstsara |
| orange | ts'ee-moozha |
| pink | sirla-ts'ee |
| purple | sheeq'ana basäh'; fyoletovi |
| red | ts'ee |
| white | k'ai |
| yellow | moozha |

## 27. SPORTS

Displays of physical strength are greatly prized in Chechen society. Wrestling is a particularly favorite sport and great tournaments are held in the summer months, together with great tests of strength — similar to the spirit of the Highland Games in Scotland. More recent sports adopted include judo and other martial arts, basketball, and, of course, soccer.

| | |
|---|---|
| athletics | **atletika** |
| ball | **bürk** |
| basketball | **basketbol** |
| chess | **shakhmatash** |
| goal | **gol** |
| horse racing | **gowrash khakhkar** |
| horse-riding | **gowrah' leelar** |
| match | **mach** |
|    soccer match | **futboli mach** |
| pitch | **ploschadka** |
| rugby | **ragbi** |
| skating | **saalaz khekhkar** |
| skiing | **kogsaalazash khekhkar** |
| soccer | **futbol** |
| stadium | **stadiyon** |
| swimming | **neeka** |
| team | **komanda** |
| wrestling | **oh' tooghar lattar** |

| | |
|---|---|
| Who won? | **Toal nerg mil wu?** |
| What's the score? | **Shöt hu yu?** |

# 28. THE BODY

| | |
|---|---|
| ankle | **h'aqolg** |
| arm | **ph'ars** |
| back | **buq'a** |
| beard | **mazh** |
| blood | **ts'i** |
| body | **degh** |
| bone | **däᶜakhk** |
| bottom | **t'eeh'e;** *informal* **keg** |
| breast; chest | **naaqa** |
| chin | **ch'enga** |
| ear | **lerg** |
| elbow | **goola** |
| eye | **bᶜärg** |
| face | **yoh'** |
| finger | **p'elg** |
| foot | **kog** |
| genitals | **sten-börsha organash** |
| hair | **mesash** |
| hand | **küg** |
| head | **kort** |
| heart | **dog** |
| jaw | **mochkhal** |
| kidney | **zhim** |
|    kidneys |    **zhannash** |
| knee | **goola** |
| leg | **kog** |
| lip | **balda** |
| liver | **doᶜah'** |
| lung | **pakh** |
|    lungs |    **peekhash** |
| moustache | **meeqash** |
| mouth | **batt** |
| neck | **ghort** |
| nose | **mara** |

# THE BODY

| | |
|---|---|
| shoulder | **belsh** |
| stomach | **kiira** |
| teeth | **tsergash** |
| throat | **legash** |
| thumb | **boqqa p'elg** |
| toe | **kooga p'elg** |
| tongue | **mott** |
| tooth | **tserg** |
| vein | **dega pkha** |
| veins | **pkheenash** |
| womb | **beeran ts'a; gai** |
| wrist | **ph'ars** |

## 29. POLITICS

| | |
|---|---|
| aid worker | **gho desh volu belkhaloo** |
| ambassador | **posol** |
| arrest | **laatsar** |
| assassination *of a man* | **stag veer** |
| *of a woman* | **zuda yeer** |
| assembly | **gullam** |
| autonomy | **avtonomi** |
| cabinet | **kabinet** |
| a charity | **ghöönallin organizatsi** |
| citizen | **grazhdanin** |
| civil rights | **grazhdanski baq'oonash** |
| civil war | **grazhdanski t'om** |
| communism | **komunizm** |
| communist | **komunist** |
| concentration camp | **kontsentratsioni laager** |
| constitution | **konstitutsi** |
| convoy | **konvoi; kolonna** |
| corruption | **koruptsi** |
| coup d'état | **padchkhalkiah' kheetsam bar;** *Russian* **perevorot** |
| crime | **zulam** |
| criminal | **zulamii(n) stag** |
| crisis | **krizis** |
| dcitator | **diktator** |
| debt | **deeqar** |
| democracy | **demokrati** |
| dictatorship | **diktatura** |
| diplomatic ties | **diplomati(n) yuq'amettigash** |
| election | **kharzhamash** |
| embassy | **posolstvo** |
| ethnic cleansing | **etnicheski chistka** |
| exile | **makhkakh vaqqar** |
| free | **märsha** |
| freedom | **märshoo** |

| | | |
|---|---|---|
| government | | **pravitelstvo** |
| guerrilla | | **partizan** |
| hostage | | **zalozhnik** |
| humanitarian aid | | **gumanitarni gho** |
| human rights | | **adami(n) baq'oonash** |
| imam | | **imam** |
| independence | | **la'amalla** |
| independent | | **la'amee** |
| independent state | | **la'amee pachkhalq** |
| judge | | **südkho** |
| killer | *of a man* | **nakh boi'u stag** |
| | *of a woman* | **nakh boi'u zuda** |
| law court | | **sud** |
| law | | **nizam** |
| lawyer | | **yurist; advokat** |
| leader | | **bächcha; küigalkho** |
| left-wing | | **ärrooh'ara; levyi** |
| liberation | | **märsha vaalar** |
| majority | | **duqakha derg** |
| mercenary | | **naiyömnik** |
| minister | | **ministar** |
| ministry | | **ministerstvo** |
| minority | | **k'ezzigakh daaq'a** |
| murder | *of a man* | **stag veer** |
| | *of a woman* | **zuda yeer** |
| opposition | | **oppositsi** |
| parliament | | **parlament** |
| (political) party | | **parti** |
| politics | | **politika** |
| peace | | **masla\u1d9cat** |
| peace-keeping troops | | **masla\u1d9cat lattosh eskarsh** |
| politician | | **politik** |
| premier | | **premiyer** |
| president | | **prezident** |
| presidential guard | | **prezidentan gvardi** |
| prime minister | | **primiyer ministar** |

| | |
|---|---|
| prison | **nabakhtee** |
| prisoner-of-war | **t'eman yeesar** |
| POW camp | **t'eman yesariin laager** |
| protest | **protest** |
| rape | **(zuda) khiiza yar** |
| reactionary | **reaktsionni** |
| Red Cross | **Krasni Krest; Ts'ee Zhᶜaara** |
| refugee | **bezhenets** |
| revolution | **revolutsi** |
| right-wing | **ättooh'ara; pravyi** |
| robbery | **humnash dh'a yaqqar** |
| seat (in assembly) | **mettig; gullamyah yolu** |
| secret police | **spets sluzhba** |
| socialism | **sotsiyalizm** |
| socialist | **sotsiyalist** |
| spy | **shpiyon** |
| struggle | **q'iisam; latar** |
| theft | **q'oola; huma lachq'a yara** |
| trade union | **profsoyuz** |
| treasury | **khazna** |
| United Nations | **O.O.N. ('o-on')** |
| veto | **veto** |
| vote | **qazh** |
| vote-rigging | **qazh tasar khartsa daqqar** |
| voting | **qazh tasar** |

## 30. TIME AND DATES

| | |
|---|---|
| century | **be<sup>c</sup> sho** |
| decade | **itt sho** |
| year | **sho** |
| month | **butt** |
| fortnight | **shi k'ira** |
| week | **k'ira** |
| day (24 hour period) | **dei büüsi\*** |
| hour | **sah't** |
| minute | **minot** |
| second | **sikond** |
| | |
| dawn | **satasar** |
| sunrise | **sakhillar** |
| morning | **<sup>c</sup>üiree** |
| day | **de** |
| noon | **delq'a khan** |
| afternoon | **delq'a khan t'iah'** |
| evening | **süiree** |
| sunset | **malkhbuzu khan** |
| night | **büisa** |
| midnight | **büisana yuq'** |
| | |
| four days before | **di' de h'algha** |
| three days before | **qo de h'algha** |
| the day before yesterday | **stoomar** |
| yesterday | **selkhan** |
| last night | **siisa** |
| today | **takhan** |
| tomorrow | **qaana** |
| the day after tomorrow | **qaana <sup>c</sup>iicha; lama** |
| three days from now | **ula** |
| four days from now | **di' de dälcha** |

\* Literally 'day and night'.

| | |
|---|---|
| the year before last | **shi sho h'algha** |
| last year | **stokhka** |
| this year | **hoqa sharah'** |
| next year | **ker dooghacha sharah'** |
| the year after next | **shi sho dälcha** |
| last week | **dh'a daghnacha k'irnah'** |
| this week | **hoqa k'irnah'** |
| next week | **kera dooghacha k'irnah'** |
| this morning | **hoqa <sup>c</sup>üiran** |
| now | **hintsa** |
| tonight | **tkhowsa** |
| yesterday morning | **selkhan <sup>c</sup>üiran** |
| yesterday afternoon | **selkhan sarah'** |
| yesterday night | **siisar** |
| tomorrow morning | **qaan <sup>c</sup>üiran** |
| tomorrow afternoon | **qaan delq'khan t'iah'** |
| tomorrow night | **qaan sarah'** |
| | |
| in the morning | **<sup>c</sup>üiran** |
| in the afternoon | **delq'akhan t'iah'** |
| in the evening | **sarah'** |
| | |
| past | **khila zama** |
| present | **hara zama** |
| future | **t'e yooghu zama** |
| | |
| What date is it today? | **Takhana hu de du?** |
| What time is it? | **Mas dälla wain?** |
| It is . . . o'clock. | **. . . (sah't) dälla.** |

## SEASONS

| | |
|---|---|
| summer | **äkhkee** |
| autumn | **güiree** |
| winter | **<sup>c</sup>a; <sup>c</sup>an** |
| spring | **b<sup>c</sup>ästee** |

# TIME & DATES

**DAYS OF THE WEEK**

| Monday | **Orshot; Orshot de** |
| Tuesday | **Shinar(a); Shinari(n) de** |
| Wednesday | **Qa'ar(a); Qa'ari(n) de** |
| Thursday | **Ye'ar(a); Ye'ari(n) de** |
| Friday | **P'eerska** |
| Saturday | **Shoot** |
| Sunday | **K'iran de** |

**MONTHS**

| January | **Yanvar** |
| February | **Fevral** |
| March | **Mart** |
| April | **Aprel** |
| May | **Mai** |
| June | **Iyun** |
| July | **Iyul** |
| August | **Avgust** |
| September | **Sentyabar** |
| October | **Oktyabar** |
| November | **Noyabar** |
| December | **Dekabar** |

## 33. OPPOSITES

| | |
|---|---|
| beginning – end | **yuh'/ dh'a voolavalar – chaqqee/cheqq daalar** |
| clean – dirty | **ts'ena – böökha** |
| comfortable – uncomfortable | **parghatee – tsa parghat** |
| fertile – barren | **yalta h'eeqa – yalta tsakhülu** |
| happy – unhappy | **reeza volu – reeza vootsush** |
| life – death | **daakhar – dalar** |
| friend – enemy | **dottagh – mostagh** |
| modern – traditional | **vai(n) kheena(n) – laamasta(n)** |
| modern – ancient | **vai(n) kheena(n) – shira** |
| open – shut | **dillana – q'oilana** |
| wide – narrow | **shüüra – yütt'a** |
| high – low | **leqa – logha** |
| peace – violence/war | **maashar – t'om** |
| polite – rude | **özda – k'orshama** |
| silence – noise | **tiinalla – ghowgha** |
| cheap – expensive | **yoorakh – yeza** |
| hot/warm – cold/cool | **dowkha – shiila** |
| health – disease | **mogshalla – lazar** |
| well – sick | **mogush – tsomgush** |
| night – day | **büüsa – de(n)** |
| top – bottom | **böh' – bugha** |
| backwards – forwards | **yukha – h'alkha** |
| back – front | **t'eeh'a – h'alkha** |
| dead – alive | *m* **vella/** *f* **yella – diina** |
| near – far | **ulläh' – geenah'** |
| left – right | **äroo – ättoo** |
| in – out | **chu – aara** |
| up – down | **h'ala – oh'a** |
| yes – no | **ha' – haa-ha'** |
| here – there | **quzah' – tsigah'** |
| soft – hard | **k'eeda – ch'oogha** |
| easy – difficult | **atta – khala** |

| | |
|---|---|
| quick – slow | **sikha – mellish** |
| big – small | **doqqa – zhima** |
| old – young | **q'eena – zhima** |
| tall – short | **leqa – dootsu** |
| strong – weak | **ch'oogha – ghiila** |
| success – failure | **ättoo – ätto tsa khilar** |
| new – old | **kellä – tisha** |
| question – answer | **khattar – zhop** |
| safety – danger | **qeramzalla – qeram** |
| good-bad | **dika(nig) – vo(n)** |
| true–false | **niisa – kharts** |
| light-heavy | **dai(n) – deza** |
| light *noun* – dark *noun* | **daala – boda** |
| well – badly | **dika – vo(n)** |
| truth – lie | **baq'derg – äshpash; püchash** |

For background on the history, culture and traditions of the Chechens there is *The Chechens: A Handbook* (Peoples of the Caucasus Series, Caucasus World, published by Curzon Press, London). For political developments, read *The Chechen Struggle for Independence*, by Marie Bennigsen Broxup and Moshe Gammer (Hurst, London), *Pride of Small Nations: The Caucasus and Post-Soviet Disorder*, by Suzanne Goldenberg (Zed Books, London).

There are also excellent up-to-date printed reports from the Radio Liberty bulletins as well as pressure groups such as Amnesty International, International Alert and the Minority Groups Report. A good source of general information is also the UNPO (Unrepresented Nations and Peoples Organization) based in The Hague in the Netherlands. For a good historical overview of the area there is *Shamil and the Conquest of Chechnya and Daghestan*, by Moshe Gammer (Frank Cass, London) and the reprint of *The Russian Conquest of the Caucasus*, by J. P. Baddeley (Caucasus World, Curzon Press, London).

For further study into the language, the best place to start would be Johanna Nichols' two sketches of Chechen and Ingush in *The Indigenous Languages of the Caucasus – Volume 4: North East Caucasian Languages*, edited by Rieks Smeets (Caravan Books, New York). For those with a knowledge of Russian there are the two excellent dictionaries: *Chechensko-Russkii slovar'*, by A.G. Matsiev, and *Russko-Chechenskii Slovar'*, by A. T. Karasayev and A. G. Matsiev (both published in Moscow).

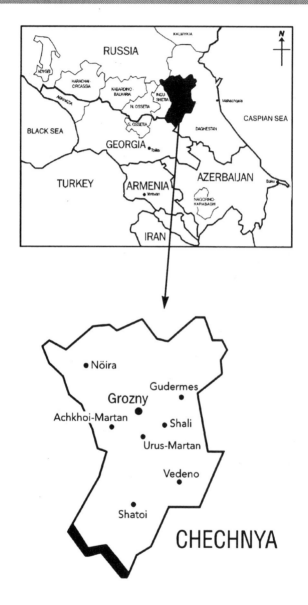

Maps by Emanuela Losi